Teaching modern languages

The Open University Postgraduate Certificate of Education

The readers in the PGCE series are:

Thinking Through Primary Practice
Teaching and Learning in the Primary School
Teaching and Learning in the Secondary School
Teaching English
Teaching Mathematics
Teaching Science
Teaching Technology
Teaching Modern Languages
Teaching History

All of these readers are part of an integrated teaching system; the selection is therefore related to other material available to students and is designed to evoke critical understanding. Opinions expressed are not necessarily those of the course team or of the University.

If you would like to study this course and receive a PGCE prospectus and other information about programmes of professional development in education, please write to the Central Enquiry Service, PO Box 200, The Open University, Walton Hall, Milton Keynes, MK7 6YZ. A copy of *Studying with the Open University* is available from the same address.

Teaching modern languages

Edited by Ann Swarbrick
at The Open University

London and New York
in association with
The Open University

First published 1994
by Routledge
11 New Fetter Lane, London EC4P 4EE

Simultaneously published in the USA and Canada
by Routledge
29 West 35th Street, New York, NY 10001

Selection and editorial matter: © 1994 The Open University

Typeset in Garamond by Florencetype Ltd, Kewstoke, Avon
Printed and bound in Great Britain by
Biddles Ltd, Guildford and King's Lynn

British Library Cataloguing in Publication Data
A catalogue record for this book is available from the British Library.

Library of Congress Cataloging in Publication Data
Teaching modern languages/edited by Ann Swarbrick.
   p.   cm.
Includes bibliographical references and index.
1. Languages, Modern – Study and teaching.   I. Swarbrick, Ann.
PB35.T433   1994
418'.007 – dc20   93–1712
                                            CIP

ISBN 0–415–10255–3

Contents

Foreword

The form of teacher education is one of the most debated educational issues of the day. How is the curriculum of teacher education, particularly initial, pre-service education to be defined? What is the appropriate balance between practical school experience and the academic study to support such practice? What skills and competence can be expected of a newly qualified teacher? How are these skills formulated and assessed and in what ways are they integrated into an ongoing programme of professional development?

These issues have been at the heart of the development and planning of the Open University's programme of initial teacher training and education – the Postgraduate Certificate of Education (PGCE). Each course within the programme uses a combination of technologies, some of which are well tried and tested, while others, on information technology for example, may represent new and innovatory approaches to teaching. All, however, contribute in an integrated way towards fulfilling the aims and purposes of the course and programme.

All of the PGCE courses have readers which bring together a range of articles, extracts from books, and reports that discuss key ideas and issues, including specially commissioned chapters. The readers also provide a resource that can be used to support a range of teaching and learning in other types and structures of course.

This series from Routledge, in supporting the new Open University PGCE programme, provides a contemporary view of developments in primary and secondary education and across a range of specialist subject areas. Its primary aim is to provide insights and analysis for those participating in initial education and training. Much of its content, however, will also be relevant to ongoing programmes of personal and institutional professional development. Each book is designed to provide an integral part of that basis of knowledge that we would expect of both new and experienced teachers.

Bob Moon
Professor of Education, The Open University

Introduction

Ann Swarbrick

This book is largely concerned with learners and teachers of Modern Foreign Languages (MFL) in secondary schools in the UK. It attempts to draw out some, not all, of the issues currently being debated in the world of MFL education. It explores aspects of learning such as 'communication', 'differentiation', 'autonomy', 'role play' and 'creativity'. Terms such as these tend to infiltrate the language of education, are interpreted in superficial ways, quickly become jargon, and eventually lose their original meaning and purpose. They become shorthand for teachers. But such terms are part and parcel of the revolution in languages education which has taken place in recent years under the banner of 'the communicative approach'. They become clichés only if teachers do not participate in the debate and simply accept the gospel which is handed down. Unless teachers take ownership of these ideas they will remain clichés. This book attempts to give a clear definition of the issues which preoccupy language teachers today to encourage readers to enter into the dialogue and challenge it from a rational and theoretical standpoint. It attempts to set MFL education in its historical perspective, to investigate and sharpen our definition of 'communicative', to consider the implications this has for the classroom and finally to suggest ways of exploiting the creative potential of learners to give them a clearer notion of what it is to communicate with a speaker of another language.

In Part I William Rowlinson and Barry Jones uncover the roots of present developments to show that, though some approaches and techniques move in and out of favour, they are not 'back of an envelope jobs' but have evolved through centuries of thought, the suggestion being that there is no such thing as a new idea in language teaching!

Part II takes a closer took at what is meant by 'the communicative approach'. Rosamond Mitchell introduces its social and linguistic origins, outlines its main tenets, discusses some issues which remain unresolved and suggests ways forward for classroom practice. This is followed by a chapter by David Little, Seán Devitt and David Singleton, which applies the principles of the communicative approach to the use of the authentic text (a text 'created to fulfil some social purpose in the language community in which it was produced'). They suggest that the communicative classroom can only provide a truly 'acquisition rich environment' if attention is paid to the types of texts learners are given to read. The writers offer a strong justification for this.

Francis Debyser's chapter is one of two in the book written in French. It is a defence of the communicative approach, claiming that it has brought foreign language learning a long way from the strict grammar-oriented pedagogy defined by Rowlinson in the first article. The movement has carried with it a return to meaning, less repetition, an emphasis on the learner and attention to the social and pragmatic aspects of communication.

Michael Grenfell questions how far we have gone down the road which Debyser has described for us. He suggests that the GCSE, which has profoundly affected practice in many classrooms, is no more than 'a transactional wolf in a communicative sheep's clothing'. He attempts to suggest why present practice is often not as effective as we would hope.

Keith Morrow, who specialises in English as a foreign language, concludes Part II. He discusses what constitutes a mistake in communicative language teaching and whether mistakes matter, arguing that we need a clear view of this if the communicative movement is to develop further.

Part III is set firmly in the classroom and discusses different issues in the context of present classroom practice. The first chapter, by Bernadette Holmes, is on differentiation. She begins by defining the ways in which pupils differ, differentiation being the process by which we recognise and respond to differences. She then discusses how teachers can plan for differentiation and gives examples of differentiated classroom activities linked to the four national curriculum attainment targets (listening, speaking, reading and writing). She gives a clear description of the conditions necessary for this type of learning to take place. This provides a useful preamble to David Little's discussion of autonomy in language learning. This is a short piece defining what autonomy is and is not, and raising the issue of practical considerations for the teacher.

The discussion in the previous two chapters begs the question of how, specifically, teachers cater for learners with difficulties. This is discussed by Barbara Lee, who outlines the findings of an NFER (National Foundation for Educational Research) project. She offers practical advice from teachers of both MFL and Special Educational Needs in mainstream secondary education, and from teachers in special schools.

Earl Stevick discusses the difference between acquiring and learning a language. He focuses on memory and how, if we take language out of a natural context as, for example, in language practice drills, we rob the learner of important memory triggers and this hinders both learning and acquisition.

Iain Mitchell takes the notion of the '*bain linguistique*' and suggests ways of sustaining it in the classroom. He considers the conditions necessary to encourage both teacher-pupil and pupil-pupil interaction in the foreign language. The issue of using the foreign language as the main medium of communication in the classroom is discussed further, in the more specific context of grammar teaching, by Theodore Kalivoda. He proposes a combined implicit and explicit approach to Spanish grammar teaching in which the teacher uses Spanish exclusively over most of the class time, then uses English at the end of the lesson to confirm and clarify understanding. In the short chapter that follows, Brian Page considers language teaching objectives, the notion of accuracy and the communicative value of correct grammar.

Part III concludes with an article by Paul McGowan and Maggie Turner outlining ways of systematically helping learners to develop their reading skills in MFL. They argue that it is not simply a matter of providing texts for learners but that we need to rethink our approach to the whole issue.

Some teachers believe that despite the revolution of the communicative method and the introduction of the GCSE, language teaching is, nevertheless, in the doldrums. Syllabuses are all too often topic bound, offering no outlet for learners to be creative in their language use. How this has come about is difficult to know since, as we have seen from Part II of this book, the communicative approach strives to encourage that very creativity which seems to be lacking. The final part of this book suggests that it is important to appeal to the imagination of learners if they are to find their wings and fly.

Part IV opens with my own chapter about the forgotten world of creative writing. It attempts to give a rationale for developing learners' writing skills and it offers practical advice on how to encourage the particular skill of poetry writing in the foreign language.

The chapter by Alan Maley and Alan Duff enters the world of drama. It outlines a strong argument for developing drama techniques in the MFL classroom, presenting this discipline as the one area of the curriculum which does not respect subject barriers. Drama is 'like the naughty child who climbs the high walls and ignores the "No Trespassing" sign'.

In the following chapter on simulations, written in French, Jean-Marc Caré disputes the argument that learners must be totally prepared for every situation they might encounter before they are able to take risks or be spontaneous. He argues that if learners habitually sit behind desks in their early years as foreign language learners, they will quickly reach inertia and any spontaneity they might have had will be stifled.

The book concludes with Barrie Joy's chapter on role. He redefines the term within a sociolinguistic and psychological frame of reference, encouraging teachers to take a new look at the creative possibilities it offers to learners and underlining the importance of cultural awareness in MFL teaching.

It is the intention of this book to raise issues currently being debated in MFL education and to offer a rationale for many of the developments taking place in schools under the influence of the national curriculum. But words and rational arguments are meaningless unless they affect what is going on in the classroom. I hope that the book will be a source of inspiration to readers and will play an important part in encouraging innovation in MFL class-rooms today.

Part I

The historical ball and chain

Chapter 1

The historical ball and chain

William Rowlinson

It is easy, and rather dangerous, to view language-teaching methodology, and indeed other aspects of education also, as a continuous upward progress through history. This view recognises that there have been occasional set-backs and difficulties, but generally sees an upward path illuminated by growing scientific insight and culminating in today's practice, not yet perfect but moving towards perfection. Involved in this attitude is the occasional not too precise glance at assumptions, approaches, methods, courses, sylla-buses, examinations of previous times, followed by pious astonishment that their perpetrators could be so obtuse, out-of-touch, ill-informed, or down-right foolish. But in fact a closer reading of older books on language teaching may well surprise: you may be struck by how much there is, once you have allowed for those often trivial matters and attitudes which are specific to the age, that coincides with modern ideas. Read Jespersen or Comenius and you find yourself constantly saying 'But I thought that was a new idea.' And these two have much in common with each other, over 250 years, as well as with modern ideas.

Methodologies are as much a product of their times as educational systems, and equally rooted in the ideas of their time. Ideas, too, have a habit of coming into and going out of fashion. What is taught and how it is taught is a product of these ideas, as well as of the conditions in which it is to be taught. It is society that determines the content of education, in the light of the dominant philosophy and (more recently) scientific concept. Many, perhaps most, new approaches are rediscoveries of old methods neglected and left in the shade, now re-illuminated by the light of social need. Language teaching, like all other teaching, reflects the temper of the times.

In medieval Europe the foreign language taught was Latin: before the thirteenth century no languages other than Latin and Greek were formally taught. Latin, though, was not just a lingua franca; it was the key to the world of scholarship and, from the Renaissance on, to the classical treasure-house of learning. There was a model for this medieval position of Latin in the role of Greek in ancient Rome itself. Then, ironically, Latin was the relatively despised vernacular and Greek the key to all learning, literature, philosophy. The cultivated Roman, like the medieval scholar, had to be bilingual.

The rise of the vernaculars and their diffusion through the new technology of printing meant a gradual separation of functions: Latin was still the key to literature and thought, the essential tool for any sort of education, but more and more through the fifteenth, sixteenth and seventeenth centuries the vernacular took over its social role as a language of everyday communication. Gradually Latin ceased to be taught as, say, English is taught in India and became a thing apart from society in general. So methods were adapted to roles. Modern languages, where taught, were taught by oral methods for communicative purposes; Latin (and Greek) mainly by book methods for literary and philosophical use.

The most famous language teacher and methodologist of this time was the Moravian J.A. Comenius (1592–1670) and it is significant that his concern was initially with the teaching of Latin and his works were written in Latin. An ecclesiastic as well as a teacher, which was not unusual for his time, Comenius was unusual for the time in that he had had some training as a teacher and his writings are derived from his own experience. His works stress the importance of the senses, their role in combination with the word in understanding and retention, and the importance of physical activity in the classroom. He is best known for his use of pictures in language teaching, but in fact he saw them only as a substitute for the real thing. His *Orbis sensualium pictus* (1654) is often cited as a forerunner of the audio-visual method: it is in fact a sequence of numbered picture vocabularies (in Latin plus three vernaculars, German, Hungarian and Czech). It may equally be seen as the forerunner of the disposable workbook (Comenius wanted the pupils to colour in the illustrations) at a time when textbooks of any kind were still scarce in the classroom, and for all the pupils in a class to have the same textbook was a rarity.

Much in Comenius is quite surprisingly modern:

> The exemplar should always come first, the precept should always follow, and imitation should always be insisted on.[1]

> The short before the long, the simple before the complex, the general before the particular, the nearer before the more remote, the regular before the irregular.[2]

Comenius in his early works sees language in use as the starting point, reality as all-important, grammar as secondary and the language classroom as a place where the senses rather than the mind come first. 'The Comenian classroom was one in which both teacher and pupils were in constant activity.'[3] And yet by the end of his life Comenius had himself done a volte-face, was renouncing his earlier methods and was proposing the derivation of language by the learner from a pre-learned set of rules of grammar. What had happened? Was this simply a step towards reaction in an old man?

What had in fact happened was the dawn of the Age of Reason. Comenius stands at a watershed, at the end of the dominance of the Renaissance view of life, of education, and especially of the Renaissance view of the role of Latin.[4] The Renaissance man was a doer, the seventeenth- and eighteenth-century man was a thinker. Language for the Cartesian man of reason was governed by the same logic that governed all things: the basic rules of one language were the same as those of all languages. They were embedded in its grammar and the art of translation was a central one, involving the manipulation of universals. Surface appearances might be different, underlying laws were essentially the same.[5] The grammar-translation method was born as a new, insightful way of approaching language learning that was exactly in tune with the times, with their emphasis on the primacy of reason, law, logic. It superseded the older more pragmatic oral approaches because its apparent precision and universality gave it a prestige in the eyes of an age that valued these qualities highly. Interestingly, it first made its way in the teaching of modern languages, with the classics (where it eventually became most firmly entrenched) adopting its precepts and methods whole-heartedly only at the start of the nineteenth century. In Britain the pre-eminence it retained through the nineteenth century was related to the ethos of an education system geared to the development of logical thinking and to teaching an élite of cultivated minds.

Modern foreign languages, as well as the classics, as taught in the schools of the nineteenth century, could hardly be justified in utilitarian terms for empire-builders or industrialists in what was clearly the most important country in the world: in such terms they were merely for the specialist. But as part of the development of the mind, a continuation of the eighteenth century's placing of logic, scientific logic, in the central position, there was much sense in language learning and language manipulation through a set of grammar rules that brought logic and as far as possible universal applicability to the fore. And methods were tailored to these ends. If modern languages were seen as inferior to classical ones in these terms it was not only because the classics still gave access to the great storehouse of literary and philosophical models, but also because the classical languages, being dead, could not be interfered with by inconsiderate foreigners who actually spoke them, altered them, and often refused to follow the rules of the grammar book. They were more easily treated as a self-contained system.

It was the rise of universal education (and especially, in Britain, the growth of the maintained grammar schools as a result of the 1902 Act) that began the swing of the pendulum in the twentieth century back towards a more pragmatic, more communicative approach. There were movements already in this direction on the continent, fuelled by the newly developed 'science' of phonetics and its apologist Henry Sweet, and by popularisers such as Viëtor, whose pamphlet 'Die Sprachunterricht muß umkehren' (1882) became the bible of the evangelists of the New or Direct (or a dozen other similar attributives) Method.

Seen on this sort of time-scale the various movements and methods of the twentieth century come together as a single reaction, more in tune with the pragmatism and the educational democracy of the times, turning away from reason, the mind, law and logic as the highest goods. Moreover, they are moving not so much forward as round to the Renaissance position, so that Comenius's earlier writings are rediscovered as startlingly consonant with the position that has now been reached.[6] In these terms the twentieth-century experience can be seen not so much as a group of radicals battling with reactionaries, as the rediscoverers of Renaissance man fighting the inheritors of the age of Reason.

Let us now look at our twentieth-century battles in more detail, for it is only in this way that we can see why one textbook is so heavily weighted towards structure drills, why another course has no textbook at all, why this examination is heavy on multiple-choice tests, why that one still insists on the virtue of prose translation. And we may perhaps see that we are not on a broad uphill road to better and better methodology and more and more efficient teaching, but that methods and materials are necessarily a reflection of aims and purposes which in turn lie in the changing structure and values of the society around us.

The label that has survived today from the nineteenth century is the Direct Method. In content it seems to go back to J.S. Blackie, a Scottish classics teacher who in the 1850s was advocating (one might say re-advocating) the avoidance of the mother tongue, the direct association of word with object, and the relegation of grammar to a subordinate position.[7] The new method attempted to legitimate itself by reference to the way a child learns its first language,[8] but it was phonetics which appeared to give both a scientific respectability and also a way round the doubtful and difficult orthography of the printed word and the attendant stress on reading and writing. Above all it seemed to provide easy classroom access to communication in society rather than to literature in the study.

At first the reform methods made slow progress. From the central place that language learning had had in the medieval and Renaissance curricula, it had by the nineteenth century been pushed to the periphery, partly because its aims had remained unchanged from those of the eighteenth century, as had its methods, largely grammar-translation. Thus nothing obviously relevant was being taught, and the 'mental discipline' aspect of the work, central to the approach and method originally, was felt to be far better catered for by classics and mathematics. Those modern language teachers who were concerned to transform their discipline in the direction of language for communication came together for the first time in a national conference in 1890 and two years later formed the Modern Languages Association. This was something of a turning-point for the new methods in Britain. The teachers were inspired by the German debate surrounding Viëtor's pamphlet (Viëtor himself addressed the 1890 conference) and passed resolutions supporting oral work, direct method and the use of phonetics.

The turn of the century also produced notable and influential publications. Sweet's *The Practical Study of Languages* (1899) is particularly concerned to deny the 'universal rule' ideas of Cartesian thought that, however debased, underlay the grammar-translation methods of his time. Exposure to the language is the banner he fights under, with phonetics as his big guns. The language comes first: 'listen before you imitate', phonetics allows precise recording of what is heard, and what *is* heard will be arbitrary, not the product of pre-learned rules. The work is a clear pointer to the behaviourist approaches of the audio-lingual school, but also, in its insistence on a broad exposure to language, a pointer, too, to some of the criticisms made of them.

However, the man whose name is most closely associated with the Direct Method is Otto Jespersen, Professor of English at the University of Copenhagen, whose book *Sprogundervisning* (translated into English in 1904 as *How to Teach a Foreign Language*) had tremendous success. The *Academy* magazine wrote of a later edition of it 'The Reform method of teaching has prevailed and to no one is more honour due for the victory than the distinguished Danish linguist and teacher, Dr Otto Jespersen.' And in fact its successes included the adoption of this method as the sole one to be used in schools by France, Belgium and Germany. This book is an easily read, common-sense, practical work that assumes communication as an end and suggests a range of means, most of which would be acceptable to the modern comprehensive school teacher with the same end in view (the notable exception is the stress on phonetics). Like Comenius's work, Jespersen's book seems surprisingly modern only because similar aims tend to produce similar methods. He advocates natural, useful language material, careful listening, direct association of word with object or idea, grammar derived from language known, and the foreign language as the principal if not only means of communication in the classroom.

The Direct Method in fact failed in Britain (though not in Germany) for a number of reasons. Circular 797 of 1912 of the Board of Education ('Modern Languages') reporting on it, says categorically 'the staff is unequal to the task'. But it is also clear that the task was misunderstood. Phonetic script (the technological panacea of the time) was introduced by many schools, but not the aim of communicative ability, and thus only some of the precepts and methods of the reformers were adopted and mixed with the traditional approach. There was some excuse for this, since the schools were of necessity working towards traditional examinations. It is probably true to say that the Direct Method did not fail in England: it was never properly tried. And if there was in the first years of the century a growing public concern to improve language teaching for communication, the trauma of the First World War changed this almost completely.

The chauvinism produced by the war in a generation of schoolchildren and their teachers for perhaps a dozen years from 1914 enabled those forces to triumph that were concerned to maintain language teaching in the literary/mental discipline mode. These were above all the universities, both in the context of their own courses and the implied prerequisites for them, and in their control of the new School Certificate and Higher School Certificate examinations from 1917 onwards. The teaching force, too, was weakened by the wholesale slaughter of the war years, but even more, public opinion became inward-looking, anti-European and especially anti-German. Language learning in the schools reflected this and language as abstract logic gained in respectability.

However, the movement towards language for communication was still there, though battered. In Harold Palmer it had a new guru. His *Scientific Study and Teaching of Languages* (1917) and later works such as *The Principles of Language Study* (1922) and *This Language-learning Business* (with H.V. Redman, 1932) discarded pure Direct Method, pointing out its fallacies, and liberated the teacher from her most difficult (and perhaps impossible) task, the conveyance of meaning entirely in the foreign language. At the same time Palmer's approach allowed and encouraged her in strategies for maximising teaching efficiency still with communication as her goal.

Palmer saw the need to fit the language course to the aims of the actual students rather than some abstract goal: 'We cannot design a language course until we know something about the students for whom the course is intended, for a programme of study depends on the aim or aims of the students. All we can say in advance is that we must endeavour to utilize the most appropriate means to attain the desired end.'[9] Palmer was suspicious of panaceas, of uncritical acceptance of one right way in anything; none the less, he believed in the need for exposure to the language, and advocated the pupils' complete immersion in the foreign language for a period before being allowed to use it. He himself exposed his pupils to the foreign language for three months before allowing them to use it.[10] To Palmer we also owe the first large-scale and systematic working-out and use of the pattern drill. Palmer was the first person to point out the difference between intensive and extensive reading and to draw lessons from this for the language classroom including the use of silent reading. He was consciously eclectic: method was 'the multiple line of approach'.[11] But he differentiated between 'studial' approaches to language learning and unconscious assimilation, realising that what coursebook and teacher intend is different from what each individual pupil learns. In this he goes a long way towards the important distinction made by Stephen Krashen[12] between the imposed process of Learning and the self-organised, subconscious process of Acquisition. None the less, overall Palmer relies heavily on habit-forming drills designed to ensure 'automatism'. He is aware of the potential monotony of this, but not much attention is paid to ways of motivating the student to use, actively and realistically, the language he has acquired. Palmer's six basic principles were: 1. ears before eyes; 2. reception before reproduction; 3. oral repetition before reading (he means reading aloud); 4. immediate memory before prolonged memory (proficiency in the 'just-heard' is most important); 5. chorus work before individualised work; 6. drill work before free work. There are certainly echoes of Comenius here!

Palmer's ideas were generally practical and represented a considerable step in the direction of communication. Movement in this direction was also helped by the fact that as the effects of the war became less immediate, public opinion gradually became more outward-looking. And now there were more language graduates teaching in the schools. These were, however, products of university courses with a mental-training plus literary criticism approach which left them uninformed about the foreign country and in-capable in the oral language. The skills they had, though, fitted the examin-ations available, which were almost exclusively of the printed and written word. Inter-war textbooks might nod towards the Direct Method (and indeed one of the more popular ones, Mrs Saxelby's French Course,[13] did a good deal more than nod) but classroom methods still consisted largely of: read aloud, translate into English, expound the grammar, write the test exercises and, culmination, translate back into French.

The Second World War had an opposite effect to that of the First. Thanks largely to American military experience, new methods geared to new aims came to a postwar Britain that became more rapidly outward-looking than after World War One. In particular there had been a leap forward in technology. Wartime gramophones might be useful for playing records to the sixth form, but after the war the movable, if not easily portable, tape-recorder and the reasonably reliable film-strip projector meant that a use-threshold of the technology had been crossed: it could be fitted by an enthusiastic teacher into her everyday teaching without too much difficulty. Just as important, a new theory of language learning and the course materials to go with it were there.

The new approach was based on behaviourist ideas of learning. These saw language – spoken language – as a collection of habits, and language teaching as habit formation. The amount of language to which the learner was exposed was to be strictly limited but unsimplified; real language with real intonation at real speed. It was to be 'overlearned' by repetition so that it became automatic, and was not to be analysed grammatically (there was no grammar progression in the early courses) but manipulated by the substi-tution of items in 'open' slots in the utterance: *Je te l'ai déjà // envoyé/ emprunté/donné . . . J'aurais bien voulu // des poires/une carte postale/un verre d'eau. . . .* The tape-recorder was essential to provide the repeated models for pupil repetition. With only a tape-recorder the method was termed 'audio-lingual'; with the addition of film-strip still-pictures to give instant recognition of the 'meaning' of the utterance (i.e. the context in which it could be effectively uttered) the method became 'audio-visual'.

The TAVOR[14] course produced at SHAPE headquarters in Paris to teach French to non-French-speaking personnel of NATO forces was the first audio-visual course to become available in British schools, in the late 1950s. It was based on the behaviourist principles just stated, with language load very heavily reduced and overlearning through much repetition (each phrase was parroted three times) central to classroom work. It concentrated on spoken production of a limited but useful range of French, with stress on exact intonation, normal (or at least near-normal) speed, real French expressions (or so they appeared in comparison with what was otherwise available), and with no grammar progression or simplification of the language in the early stages of learning. By concentrating on a limited area of one skill and hammering this through new technology, the course appeared to work. The mindnumbing effect of the constant repetition was alleviated initially by the positive motivation produced by the novelty of the equipment: specially darkened rooms, tape-recorders, coloured cartoons projected on a screen. But whereas this was originally designed as material to be used in classrooms in Paris where the world of French culture began at the classroom door and where the French learned could be immediately applied just along the road to buy postcards or get a drink, in the English school situation this was not the case. Teachers mesmerised by the technology made little or no attempt to set up classroom situations where the overlearned structures might be needfully, autonomously used (this is the most difficult and often the most neglected part of foreign language teaching anyway). The accent, the speed, the intonation, the impressive Frenchness of the language learned were all there to prove that it worked (and were not these all areas that had so often been criticised in the past?). But gradually it became clear that a year or longer spent on TAVOR (or the other basic audio-visual courses that followed it) meant little more than a command of only those snippets of language that had been overlearned in the classroom. There was no transfer, no ability to develop or recombine them, no ability to generate further language. A small part of the language-learning process involving often neglected skills had been concentrated on without the realisation of *how* small a part this was and how much more there was to language teaching and learning than this; how much had in fact been neglected. Gradually this was realised and the audio-visual 'method' was dropped.[15]

Its demise was hastened by criticisms of the behaviourist learning theory that underpinned it. The central figure of behaviourist psychology in terms of its application to language learning was B.F. Skinner. From 1959 criticism of his work and theory by Noam Chomsky[16] and his followers produced an alternative approach that stressed language as rule-governed behaviour and suggested that the mechanism for formulation of these rules to generate 'new' language was a good deal more subtle than mere habit-formation. In teaching terms[17] this meant exposure to a great deal more of the language than the behaviourists were prepared to admit, much more opportunity for use by pupils of their own acquired store of the foreign language for purposes that they perceived as their own, and a view of error that saw it not as something to be avoided at all costs but as something to be learnt from, with fluency a higher good than accuracy.

A further technological 'breakthrough' of the late 1960s was the language laboratory, seductive in its apparent individualisation of learning and the consequent intensification of individual effort, and impressive as a status symbol, giving language teaching in the school something of the kudos of chemistry or physics. Again, apparently effective when the machinery was new and motivation high by reason of its novelty value, it proved inefficient, dehumanising, and, as with the audio-visual course, led to concentration on one small formal aspect of language. Most of the work done in the laboratory was again based on the Skinnerian view of operant conditioning as basic to language learning, with overlearning of structures, this time through the four-phase drill, and again at the expense of the generation of personal language by the student. It proved to be an even more costly failure than the audio-visual 'method'.[18]

It is easy to be sceptical after the event, but the teachers who showered enthusiasm on the audio-visual method or the language laboratory were genuinely concerned to realign language teaching. There was, indeed still is, a feeling that society now requires school-taught language to be of some use in real transactions, that shortening lines of communication throughout the world should be accompanied by the learning of language for use rather than as 'mental discipline'. These teachers may have been infatuated with a device, deluded by 'experts', or taken in by the novelty effect of their new approach, but they were genuinely seeking to reorient classroom language teaching (and finding it more difficult than they expected). The primary school French movement was another light that failed, another unsuccessful but nevertheless gallant attempt to turn language teaching towards new aims.

But out of all these apparent failures (and it should be stressed that none of them was a total failure), there has come one success at least. It has become clear that fascination with cleverly developed means is not a substitute for precise definition of ends, of a clear view of what 'foreign language learning' should represent for a particular child, both along the way in terms of his or her development and at the end in terms of what he or she is left with from the school foreign language classes on finally quitting them for good. Her Majesty's Inspectors in 1977, considering problems in modern languages, wrote of 'insufficiently differentiated objectives' and the need to 'offer pupils a terminal objective that they can perceive for themselves'.[19] In their report of the same year on modern languages in comprehensive schools they wrote 'Much of the underperformance revealed in this report results from a tacit assumption that all pupils studying a modern language have basically the same needs. It is abundantly clear, however, that such an assumption is not only false but has unfortunate, often distressing, consequences for many of them'.[20]

This is all part of a growing emphasis on specifying ends, of starting not from a theory of language learning that may well be superseded or drop from fashion, nor from innovations in means that appear to revolutionise teaching methods. Defined ends as the overriding factor, and means justified only in their effectiveness towards reaching these ends, correspond to the utilitarian spirit of the age. This is, for example, at the heart of the Graded-Objectives movement, which is concerned with ends rather than means and relies on eclecticism rather than fanaticism to achieve its ends.[21] But focusing on the specific ends in modern language teaching for individual learners inevitably raises questions of the role of language learning within the whole curriculum, both as this is provided overall by the school and as it is experienced individually by the various members of that school.

NOTES

1 *Novissima linguarum methodus*, 1648, quoted in Jelinek V. ed. *The Analytic Didactic of Comenius* Chicago 1953.
2 ibid.
3 Kelly L.G. *25 Centuries of Language Teaching* Rowley, Mass. Newbury House 1969 p. 11.
4 In England the watershed has been dated specifically to the Restoration (1660), which brought a French-speaking court to this country and effectively finished Latin, already dying, as the language of scholars and diplomats.
5 All of which sounds surprisingly like modern mentalist views of language acquisition. One of Noam Chomsky's more accessible and less well-known works is titled *Cartesian Linguistics*. Plus ça change . . .?
6 *Orbis sensualium pictus* was reprinted in an English edition in 1887.
7 Blackie J.S. *On the Studying and Teaching of Languages* Edinburgh 1852.
8 With this emphasis it was usually called the Natural Method. Its main advocate was the Frenchman F. Gouin, whose *L'art d'enseigner* was published in 1880. Translated into English in 1892, the work had some impact in its plea for a return in second-language learning to methods a child employs in learning its first language. Sweet amongst others pointed out the fallacy in assuming that the adolescent or adult learning a second language starts from a similar position to the child learning its mother tongue. More recently McLaughlin has made clear that the impression that we learn our first language in about four years simply is not true. Verbal comprehension reaches 80% of adult competence only at age eighteen. (McLaughlin B. *Second Language Acquisition in Childhood* Hillsdale N.J. 1978 p. 55.)
9 Palmer H.E. *The Principles of Language Study* Harrap 1922, reissued O.U.P. 1964.
10 Kelly L.G. op. cit. p. 62.
11 Palmer H.E. op. cit. p. 113.
12 Krashen S. *Second Language Acquisition and Second Language Learning* Pergamon 1981.

13 Saxelby E. *Cours de Français* Ginn 1936. It included separately published phonetic transcripts of the texts.

14 TAVOR is an acronym of Teachers' Audio-Visual Oral.

15 It is instructive to compare the first and second versions of the first two years of the Longman Audio-Visual Course (Moore S. and Antrobus A.L. 1966 and 1973), the only audio-visual course that retained general popularity. Even in its first version the course represents a compromise with the pure audio-visual doctrine, but it does have the audio-visual element as the central and virtually exclusive element; the second version de-emphasises it and adds many exercises aimed at stimulation of language-generation.

16 Initially in Chomsky's article: 'Skinner's *Verbal Behaviour*' in *Language* 35,1 (1959).

17 The mentalists were much more wary about the direct application of their language-learning theories to teaching than the behaviourists had been. None the less their ideas were adopted where their critiques seemed to correspond to classroom experience.

18 See Green P.S. ed. *The Language Laboratory in School* Oliver and Boyd 1975 for an unambiguous account of the laboratory's lack of success with high ability boys: '(pupils using a language laboratory) showed no detectable difference over a period of three years, in either performance or attitude, from a matched group of pupils that did not use the language laboratory'. Winter R. in *The Effectiveness of the Language Laboratory in Mixed Ability Teaching in Schools* (unpub. Ph.D. thesis, University of Sheffield 1982) found it equally ineffectual with secondary beginners of both sexes across the ability range.

19 *Maths, Science and Modern Languages in Maintained Schools in England* HMI 1977 p. 2.

20 *Modern Languages in Comprehensive Schools* (HMI series: Matters for Discussion 3) HMSO 1977 p. 47.

21 Whether computer-assisted language learning is another blind alley concerned with means at the expense of ends, it is still too early to say. Certainly there were many danger signals: in the early pioneering materials, mastery and use of the technology took precedence over what was being taught, and the aims and content of the material seemed to have little relative importance. But this could well be only a first stage of naïve enthusiasm. Certainly there is in the expanding capabilities of the microcomputer a huge technological potential that it should be possible to harness to some at least of modern language learning's current aims. See Davies G. and Higgins J. *Computers, language and language learning* CILT 1982.

Chapter 2

Modern languages
Twenty years of change

Barry Jones

INTRODUCTION

In the 1970s the teaching of modern languages seemed to be causing Her Majesty's Inspectorate (HMI) some concern. Whereas the majority of subjects in secondary schools were taught to all children no matter what their ability, only a proportion of the school population learnt a foreign language. According to an HMI report published in 1977, many comprehensive schools in a survey of eighty-three secondary schools, 'restricted the modern language to perhaps 60–80 per cent of the pupils' (DES 1977: 4). The report adds, 'By the fourth secondary year (age 14–15 years), a modern language was optional for the majority of pupils: in all types of school visited during the survey, only slightly more than a third of the pupils in this age group were still engaged in such studies' (ibid.: 8).

Much language learning, if the inspectors are to be believed, was also,

> characterised by some or all of the following features: under-performance in all four language skills; the setting of impossible or pointless tasks for average (and in particular less able) pupils and their abandonment of modern language learning at the first opportunity; excessive use of English and an inability to produce other than inadequate or largely unusable statements in the modern language; inefficient reading skills; and writing limited mainly to mechanical reproduction which was often extremely inaccurate.
>
> (DES 1977: 8)

Such was the opinion of HMI. A teacher writing in the *Audio-Visual Language Journal* in 1978 described a number of other problems, too. He analysed the situation from both his and the pupil's point of view. He wrote:

> I have been in a comprehensive school for over thirteen years, and each year I have taught CSE classes. It has been very hard work, demanding an inordinate amount of preparation and a great expenditure of energy in an attempt to motivate the apathetic core that exists in every CSE class. But

the examinations are always a bitter disappointment and a derisory return for those children who have shown interest and worked well: a grade higher than 4 is rare, even though the candidates always include children who have the potential for a 1 or 2.

(Richards 1978: 171)

From these two perspectives, pupil motivation and the examinations system seem to be at least two causes for concern especially in the teaching of foreign languages to children of moderate ability. The CSE (Certificate of Secondary Education), first introduced in 1965, and the GCE 'O' level (General Certificate of Education Ordinary level) examinations, in existence long before, compared in the diagram on p. 20 produced in 1981, seemed inappropriate and needed revision.

It was in this context of producing an examination better suited to the needs of learners of all abilities, and of motivating all children aged from 11 to 16, and especially those of average and below average ability, that the General Certificate of Secondary Education (GCSE) and Graded Objectives in Modern Languages (GOML) were developed. A combination of the new, joint 16+ examination and the GOML movement were seen by many people as realistic ways of assessing and motivating the whole ability range of pupils in secondary schools.

GRADED OBJECTIVES IN MODERN LANGUAGES

The Graded Objectives movement achieved its momentum in the 1970s. It was prompted largely by a feeling among teachers that, in the context of the proposed new 16+ examination, the majority of their pupils could not be expected to sustain their interest and motivation for five years without some formal indications of successful learning.

The principle of the five year course which must be completed before a public examination could be taken [was considered unacceptable]. The first principle of the graded objectives scheme was therefore that the traditional five year course to CSE/'O' level should be broken up into a set of shorter term objectives, each one leading to the next and each one building on its predecessor.

(Harding, Page and Rowell 1980: 3–4)

The second principle of the Graded Objectives movement was that learners should be given worthwhile and realistic tasks to do which were

(a) achievable by all abilities of learners;
(b) known to teachers and learners by being detailed and defined in advance of the tests;
(c) not related to any particular age of learner;
(d) specified in a defined syllabus.

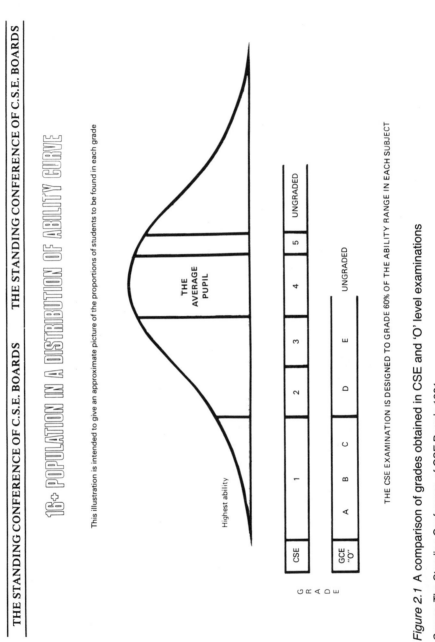

16+ POPULATION IN A DISTRIBUTION OF ABILITY CURVE

This illustration is intended to give an approximate picture of the proportions of students to be found in each grade

Highest ability

THE AVERAGE PUPIL

| CSE | 1 | 2 | 3 | 4 | 5 | UNGRADED |

| GCE "O" | A | B | C | D | E | UNGRADED |

GRADE

THE CSE EXAMINATION IS DESIGNED TO GRADE 60% OF THE ABILITY RANGE IN EACH SUBJECT

Figure 2.1 A comparison of grades obtained in CSE and 'O' level examinations

Source: The Standing Conference of CSE Boards 1981

A Graded Objectives syllabus (based on the work of Harding 1974: 163–4) was characterised by

(a) division into *receptive* (listening and reading) skills and *productive* (speaking and writing) skills;
(b) a list of the *topic areas* within each skill in which competence would be assessed.

    eg. Topic areas: 1. Speaking

      A.   PERSONAL CONVERSATION
      1. Name, age, address
      2. Family   etc.

By setting objectives which could be completed and assessed every six weeks, or on a weekly basis, or even during a single lesson, teachers found that their classes became keen to achieve the defined goals. Success was rewarded and documented. Progress was rapid. Tasks were short, defined in advance, and appeared very relevant to the learners who were frequently cast in the role of visitor to the foreign country. Certificates were awarded for different levels of achievement and most defined the language competencies which had been successfully demonstrated by the learners. Figure 2.2 shows an example from Cambridgeshire (1982).

Because some syllabuses listed the learning objectives, the language needed to fulfil them and the topics to be covered, teachers and learners had a clear idea of what was to be achieved both linguistically and thematically. Because the four language skills of listening, reading, speaking and writing were mostly assessed separately, pupils had the possibility of achieving success according to their particular language strengths. Level 1, in most schemes, did not include assessment of writing skills, and limited reading to notices, signs and very short texts, so tended to give even the weaker linguists a chance to prove that they were capable of communicating effectively at an elementary level in a limited but listed range of situations.

Much of the pioneering work of the 1970s was influential in the formulation of the national curriculum for modern foreign languages.

THE GCSE

At the same time as the graded objectives movement was establishing itself, the production of a new 16+ examination was being initiated. This new examination was to be an amalgamation of the CSE and GCE 'O' level.

In order that the new syllabuses and examinations should reflect the views of all those involved – including teachers – the first years of the 1980s saw extensive consultation exercises in every subject area. A document published by the Department of Education and Science and the Welsh Office, *Foreign Languages in the School Curriculum: A consultative paper* (DES/WO 1983),

HOMERTON COLLEGE
CAMBRIDGE

CAMBRIDGESHIRE
COUNTY COUNCIL

This is to certify that . . . .

of . . . . School

has successfully completed a range of tasks in

FRENCH at LEVEL ONE
(Details of the skills and topic areas are listed overleaf.)

Alison C. Shorrock .
Principal, Homerton College

. . . .
Chief Education Officer

Date of award: . . . .

. . . .
Head Teacher

CAMBRIDGESHIRE GRADED OBJECTIVES IN MODERN LANGUAGES

FRENCH LEVEL ONE

The holder of this Certificate has shown the ability, at a simple level, to cope successfully with the listening and speaking needed to:-

- *make personal contact with a French speaker*

- *talk about themselves, their house and home, free time and interests*

- *ask for similar information in return*

- *ask the way and understand directions*

- *go shopping*

- *order snacks and drinks*

- *express some personal needs*

- *enquire about and express some feelings and to recognise signs related to the above topics.*

Figure 2.2 Level One certificate from Cambridgeshire (1982): front and back

Source: Homerton College Cambridge, Cambridgeshire County Council

was circulated widely to schools, local education authorities, examination groups, professional associations and other interested organisations.

Subject groups were set up by the new Secondary Examinations Council to write national criteria for each subject in the school curriculum. The document *GCSE. The National Criteria: French* (DES/WO 1985) was published in the same year as a national guide to the GCSE was commissioned. Referring to the national criteria the guide states:

> the national criteria represent a consensus between the teaching profession, the Examination Boards and Groups, the users of examination results, the Secondary Examinations Council and the Government. The criteria are framed in such a way as to allow considerable freedom to Examining Groups and teachers to develop different syllabuses and schemes of assessment. They are also framed to ensure that the criteria themselves can develop and that curriculum innovation is not stifled.
>
> (Jones 1986: 5)

What then were the main features of a school course which conformed to the national criteria for French? After pilot joint GCE 'O' level and CSE examinations had been trialled in 1987, the first flurry of (Secondary Examinations Council approved) GCSE syllabuses and examinations gives some indication of the changes which had been made. These included:

content of syllabuses and courses defined in terms of
- role: interviewee, narrator etc.
- settings:
    - town and country
    - home
    - school
    - work
    - places of entertainment
    - places of public transport
    - private transport
    - at the Syndicat d'Initiative
    - shops, markets and supermarkets
    - cafés and restaurants
    - hotels, youth hostels, campsites, holiday homes
    - dentist's or doctor's surgery, chemist
    - garage and petrol station
    - bank and bureau de change
    - lost property office and police station
- topics
    - for Basic level
        - personal identification
        - house and home

> geographical surroundings
> school
> free time and entertainment
> travel
> holidays
> meeting people
> shopping
> food and drink
> weather and seasons
> accommodation
> for Higher level
> > work and future
> > emergencies
> > services
> > lost property

Within each of these,

> *precise tasks which were specified.* For example, candidates should be able to
> > describe current weather conditions
> > understand people talking about the weather and simple written weather forecasts
> > make comments about the weather in casual conversation
> > talk about the climate of their own country
> > understand simple predictions about weather conditions
> > > (from Midland Examining Group 1988)

Each syllabus also contained

- *complete vocabulary lists* with words marked for receptive or productive competence;
- *lists of structures and grammatical features* which were to be taught;
- *specimen papers* in the four skill areas of listening, speaking, reading and writing;
- *assessment procedures and criteria.*

The GCSE was thus born.

THE NATIONAL CURRICULUM FOR MODERN FOREIGN LANGUAGES

In 1988 the GCSE was in its first year. Teachers were beginning to understand how to organise their teaching in terms of specified topics and settings, defined lists of language and divisions into Basic and Higher levels. Coursebooks and collections of audio cassettes had begun to provide 'authentic' materials, and 'authentic' tasks were being devised around them. Most teachers spent time during their summer holidays or during a trip with children collecting 'realia' in the form of tickets, programmes, pamphlets, timetables – all, in the words of the national criteria for French, to meet the requirement that, 'material presented to candidates should be carefully selected authentic French' and, for Basic reading, that,

> candidates should be expected, within a limited range of clearly defined topic areas, to demonstrate understanding of public notices and signs (e.g. menus, timetables, advertisements) and the ability to extract relevant specific information from such texts as simple brochures, guides, letters and forms of imaginative writing considered to be within the experience of, and reflecting the interests of, sixteen year olds of average ability.

For Higher level reading the criteria state: 'To the range of types of text (listed under Basic reading) will be added magazines and newspapers likely to be read by a sixteen year old' (DES/WO 1985: 3).

Another reform in all schools, both primary and secondary, was, however, just about to bring about even greater changes than those experienced when GCSE came into being. In 1988 Parliament passed the Education Reform Act. This provided for the 'establishment of a National Curriculum comprising core and other foundation subjects, to be taught to all pupils of compulsory school age in maintained schools, for each of which there are to be appropriate attainment targets, programmes of study and assessment arrangements. The Act defines attainment targets as "the knowledge, skills and understanding which pupils of different abilities and maturities are expected to have by the end of each key stage" and programmes of study as "the matters, skills and processes which are required to be taught to pupils of different abilities and maturities during each key stage". The four consecutive key stages cover the years of compulsory schooling from 5 to 16' (DES/WO 1990: i), key stage 1 being for 5- to 7-year-old children, key stage 2 for ages 7 to 11, key stage 3 for ages 11 to 14 and key stage 4 for ages 14 to 16.

A national curriculum modern foreign languages working group was established in August 1989. This group published its report in July 1990. The report sought to 'represent the (working group's) unanimous view as to how the ambitious goal of making at least one modern foreign language available to virtually every secondary school pupil – and more than one to as many as possible – might be achieved' (DES/WO 1990: vii).

After a period of wide consultation – the National Curriculum Council received 562 responses to the working group's final report – a Draft Order, then the Order in its final form were published, the latter coming into force on 1 August 1992. To understand what was made statutory it is perhaps helpful to look at the sections within the Order. These are

1 The four attainment targets (ATs) of
     Listening AT1
     Speaking AT2
     Reading AT3
     Writing AT4
and their associated levels and statements of attainment. (See Figure 2.3 on p. 28.)

2 The programmes of study: part I
The headings here give indications of what is required, namely:
   - *learning and using the target language* – thus that teachers and learners must use the foreign language in class, obliging teachers therefore to ensure that what they say is, as far as possible, in the foreign language throughout all lessons in all years;
   - *developing language learning skills and awareness of language* – including the understanding of grammatical features and relationships, but more besides;
   - *developing cultural awareness*;
   - *developing the ability to work with others*;
   - *developing the ability to learn independently*.

The programmes of study: part II
Here teachers, and their schemes of work, must ensure that pupils 'explore seven Areas of Experience over the period of each key stage'. The areas of experience are

   Area A: Everyday activities
   Area B: Personal and social life
   Area C: The world around us
   Area D: The world of education, training and work
   Area E: The world of communications
   Area F: The international world
   Area G: The world of imagination and creativity.
                                                    (DES/WO 1991: 27)

In order to help teachers meet these statutory requirements the National Curriculum Council published non-statutory guidance in the form of a pack of teaching ideas which focused particularly but not exclusively on

   - the attainment targets
   - the programmes of study
   - using the target language
   - progression and its implementation
   - differentiation and its implementation
   - information technology
   - planning the curriculum

The development of pupils' ability to communicate in speech		
Level	Statements of attainment	Examples
	Pupils should be able to:	
1	a) respond very briefly to what is seen or heard.	Say 'yes', 'no'; give name and age; name objects and familiar items in pictures.
	b) imitate with approximate pronunciation and intonation.	Repeat simple questions, new words and phrases, greetings, numbers 1–10, rhymes, songs, tongue-twisters.
2	a) produce short simple responses to what is seen or heard.	Give a simple description of people, places, objects (e.g. colour, size).
	b) give and find out simple information.	Ask and answer simple questions (e.g. about themselves and their families).
	c) ask for help with comprehension.	Ask for help in relation to the task (e.g. 'I don't understand'); use stock phrases to ask 'What does – mean?' 'What's the (FL) for –?'
3	a) initiate and respond with intelligible pronunciation using memorised language.	Take part in a brief prepared 'first-meeting' conversation with someone of the same age met on holiday.
	b) adapt memorised words and phrases.	Vary statements about the opening and closing times of different institutions (e.g. the bank/post office . . . opens/closes at . . . 10.00/11.00).
	c) express feelings, likes and dislikes in simple terms.	Give short reactions (e.g. 'it's good', 'it's boring', 'I agree'; 'so do I', 'I like/dislike –').
4	a) initiate and respond in conversation or role-play on familiar topics using appropriate forms of personal address.	Ask and answer questions (e.g. about leisure activities or food preferences) using a questionnaire with other pupils and adults.
	b) give a short presentation or prompted talk on everyday activities, interests or future plans.	Speak for a short time, using notes or a prepared speech on hobbies, life at home or intended career.
	c) offer simple explanations in response to the question 'why?'	Give simple reasons for liking/ disliking different types of TV programme or school subjects.

Figure 2.3 Attainment target 2: speaking

Source: Department of Education and Science and the Welsh Office (1991) *Modern Foreign Languages in the National Curriculum*, London: HMSO

- managing the curriculum
- cross-curricular issues.

(DES 1992)

These and other related issues and practices are now being discussed, trialled and evaluated by teachers in their departments and in in-service training sessions. The profession as a body is trying hard to put the national curriculum for Modern Foreign Languages into practice.

REFERENCES

Department of Education and Science (1977) *Modern Languages in Comprehensive Schools* (HMI series: Matters for discussion 3), London: HMSO.
Department of Education and Science/Welsh Office (1983) *Foreign Languages in the School Curriculum: A consultative paper*, London: DES/WO.
Department of Education and Science/Welsh Office (1985) *General Certificate of Secondary Education. The National Criteria: French*, London: DES/WO.
Department of Education and Science/Welsh Office (1990) *Modern Foreign Languages for Ages 11 to 16*, London: DES/WO.
Department of Education and Science/Welsh Office (1991) *Modern Foreign Languages in the National Curriculum*, London: HMSO.
Harding, A. (1974) 'Defined syllabuses in modern languages', *Audio-Visual Language Journal* 12(3).
Harding, A., Page, B. and Rowell, S. (eds) (1980) *Graded Objectives in Modern Languages*, London: Centre for Information on Language Teaching and Research (CILT).
Jones, B. (1986) *GCSE French: A Guide for Teachers*, Secondary Examinations Council in collaboration with the Open University, Open University Press.
Midland Examining Group (1988) *French Defined Content and Specimen Papers for General Certificate of Secondary Education*, Midland Examining Group.
National Curriculum Council (1992) *Modern Foreign Languages Non-Statutory Guidance*, National Curriculum Council.
Richards, D. (1978) 'CSE Examinations in Modern Languages: a plea for realism' *Audio-Visual Language Journal* 16(3).
Standing Conference of CSE Boards, The (1981) *CSE The Facts*, publisher unknown.

Part II

Investigating the communicative approach

Chapter 3

The communicative approach to language teaching
An introduction

Rosamond Mitchell

INTRODUCTION

The 'communicative approach' to foreign language teaching is by now around twenty years old. It is not a tightly structured 'method' of teaching, like the French audio-visual movement of the 1960s, for example, or some commercially marketed language teaching methods of today, such as 'Suggestopedia' or the 'Silent Way'. Rather it is a broad assembly of ideas, from a range of sources (some linguistic, others more broadly educational), which have together come to be accepted as 'good practice' by many contemporary teachers.

This chapter will briefly introduce the origins of the communicative approach, outline its main tenets, and review some unsolved problems in the approach and possible directions for the future.

ORIGINS OF THE COMMUNICATIVE APPROACH

In the decades following World War II, broad changes in the world economy and in society, as well as changes in the educational systems of the developed world, led to the creation of large new publics interested in foreign language learning. The number of adults wanting to learn foreign languages for a variety of purposes – business, vocational, access to higher education – increased very greatly. At secondary school level, foreign language learning had traditionally been reserved in many countries for an élite minority, attending academically oriented schools (such as the grammar schools of Britain). But in the 1960s and 1970s, foreign language learning was extended much more widely, as part of a general movement to broaden and upgrade the content of secondary education for the population overall. In Britain, the widespread establishment of comprehensive schools led for the first time to the teaching of a foreign language to virtually all children, at least in the early years of secondary school.

This broadening of the 'market' for foreign languages created pressure for change in teaching methods and curricula, to suit the needs of non-traditional groups of learners. At the same time, changes in general educational thinking were leading to requirements that learning outcomes in all subjects be specified much more clearly, often in the form of behavioural objectives – much more precise statements of what it was expected that the learners would be able to do with the knowledge and skills they had acquired during any given course of study. Similarly, more active and experiential modes of learning (such as the use of group work) were coming into favour across the curriculum as a whole. These general educational themes again created new expectations and pressures for those concerned more specifically with the teaching and learning of foreign languages.

The rise of the communicative approach can thus be seen as the response of the language teaching profession to their new situation, and a recognition of the inadequacy of traditional 'grammar/translation' methods, and also of the 'structural' methods of the 1950s (which stressed speaking and listening but relied heavily on meaningless pattern drills and repetition), to meet the needs of their new publics. Fortunately, at the time when there was a will for change, a range of new ideas in different branches of linguistics began to offer a range of possible new solutions.

A NEW THEORY OF LANGUAGE: COMMUNICATIVE COMPETENCE

> There are rules of use without which the rules of grammar would be useless.
>
> (Dell Hymes 1972)

This now famous statement, by a linguist-cum-anthropologist who had for many years been analysing speech events in traditional societies, illustrates a definitive broadening of the concept of what it means to 'know' a language, which we owe to the still-new discipline of sociolinguistics. Hymes is responsible for first popularising the notion of 'communicative competence', a view which claims that the competent language user not only commands accurately the grammar and vocabulary of the chosen target language, but also knows how to use that linguistic knowledge appropriately in a range of social situations.

Hymes himself discussed communicative competence in very general and abstract terms, and others have tried to define it more precisely, especially with foreign language learners in mind. Michael Canale, for example, has suggested (1983) that communicative competence has the following four components:

1 Grammatical competence
  (Linguistic competence, narrowly defined – pronunciation, syntax and vocabulary);

2 Discourse competence
   (Knowledge of the rules governing the structure of longer texts, conversations etc.);
3 Sociolinguistic competence
   (Control of speech and writing styles appropriate to different situations,
   knowledge of rules of politeness etc.);
4 Strategic competence
   (Knowledge of coping strategies, which can keep communication going
   when language knowledge is still imperfect – e.g. how to negotiate
   meaning or repair misunderstandings).

A NEW MODEL FOR SYLLABUS DESIGN: FUNCTIONS AND NOTIONS

The first key influence in the development of the 'communicative approach',
then, was a redefinition in broader terms of what it means to be proficient
in a language. The second key influence has been a new way of planning syllabuses for foreign language learning – the so-called 'functional/
notional' syllabus model.

Traditionally, language learning syllabuses for schools and colleges were
structured around the grammar of the target language, dealing with categories such as noun classes or verb tenses systematically in turn. Such
traditional academic syllabuses assumed that the learner's goal was a complete, in-depth mastery of the target language, and also that the learner
would be willing to study for some years before applying practically what
had been learned. These assumptions became untenable, given the new types
of learner coming forward in the postwar years. Both for busy adult learners
with vocational needs and for new-style, less academic learners of school
age, it was realised that motivation depended largely on much more immediate 'payoff' in terms of the usefulness for practical purposes of what was
taught. A search began, therefore, for types of language syllabus which
could offer at least limited communicative ability from an early stage.

British school teachers coping with the full intake of the new comprehensive school found an initial answer within the framework of the Graded
Objectives in Modern Languages (GOML) movement (Harding, Page and
Rowell 1980). This was a grass-roots movement, which flourished in the
1970s and early 1980s, in which local groups of teachers co-operated to
develop syllabuses and methods for the early years of secondary education.
Many GOML schemes were set up, typically seeking to raise pupils' motivation through teaching language appropriate to a range of 'relevant' topics
and situations (e.g. shopping, hobbies or exchange visits), and through
frequent assessment and certification. Some of these schemes, however,
offered little more language than the learning by heart of situationally
relevant phrases and vocabulary, and failed to lead the learner systematically

to linguistic independence and creativity. Purely situational syllabuses were not the whole answer.

Perhaps surprisingly, more promising answers were found in the esoteric field of linguistic philosophy, where the concept of 'speech acts' – or in John Austin's phrase, 'how to do things with words' – was already being explored. From the linguistic philosophers, applied linguists such as David Wilkins (1972) borrowed a functional view of language. They realised that it was possible to group language items for teaching purposes not only in terms of the grammatical category to which they belonged but also in terms of the language function, or speech act, they performed. Thus, for example, a range of grammatically varied language could be taught together to exemplify functions such as 'apologising', 'thanking', 'requesting', etc.

These influences could be seen in operation in a major syllabus writing project sponsored by the Council of Europe during the 1970s and 1980s. These 'threshold level' syllabuses (e.g. Van Ek 1975) tried to spell out the language needed by beginner adult learners for vocational and social purposes, in terms of situations, language functions and semantic 'notions', as well as the more traditional dimensions of grammar, vocabulary and language skills. Later, this syllabus model was adapted for school use in a variety of countries; its influence was found in some later projects within the GOML movement, and is very obvious in British foreign language GCSE syllabuses of the 1980s.

The functional syllabus model has not been without its critics, however. Though more sophisticated and more ambitious than the situational syllabus, the functional syllabus can also lead to the rote learning of unanalysed target language phrases, and may not be the most effective way to help the learner to develop a truly personal and creative language capacity. Many socalled functional syllabuses also prove, on inspection, to have a strong traditional grammatical core, though with new labels! And the most radical critics of traditional syllabus practices argue against the necessity for any predetermined language syllabus, whether grammatical or functional. Instead, they say, the learner should be given a sequence of carefully chosen (or perhaps, negotiated) tasks to carry out through the medium of the target language, which are inherently interesting and rewarding to complete. Language learning, it is argued, will ensue as new language elements necessary for the completion of each task are encountered and assimilated. Such task-based syllabus models are currently popular for adult learners (see Breen 1987 for discussion), though they have made little impact so far on language learning in the secondary school.

METHODS AND MATERIALS

With hindsight, we can now see that the major influences shaping the early development of the communicative approach were linguistic rather than psychological in nature – a new expanded definition of what it means to 'know' a language, on the one hand, and new ways of defining the content and goals of language syllabuses on the other hand.

In themselves, these influences did not necessarily imply any change in actual teaching methods. Teachers could accommodate themselves to new goals, and to new routes through the language they were teaching, while continuing to employ a mix of traditional classroom activities: presentation and explanation of new language points, exercises and activities to provide focused practice in these points, plus feedback to the learners (praise and/or correction) to guide them as they practised. Indeed, as an example of this continuity, we can see that a well-known introduction for British teachers, Bill Littlewood's *Communicative Language Teaching* (1981), preserved a relatively traditional methodological framework of presentation–practice– exploitation.

However, while no single theory of learning was a major influence on communicative language teaching in its early stages, a range of new ideas about learning were working within the movement from the beginning, and language learning theory became a progressively more important influence in the 1980s.

First, it was argued logically that having specified with greater clarity a range of real life situations in which the learner following a functional syllabus could be expected to exercise those functions, the classroom should provide opportunities for lifelike rehearsal. It was no surprise that commu- nicative methodologies have emphasised speaking and listening skills in the classroom; indeed the audio-visual and other structural methods which preceded the communicative approach had already introduced this empha- sis. But the communicative approach has brought a new emphasis on the use of role plays and simulations in the classroom, hopefully to reproduce something of the experience of target language use in the desired contexts.

Secondly, from the 1970s onwards, ideas of 'naturalness' in the FL classroom, and the view that the foreign language learning process should model itself as far as possible on the (apparently) universally successful processes of first language acquisition, became increasingly influential. Young children learning their first language, it was argued, are interested in meanings, and in getting things done; they pay little or no conscious attention to the forms of language, and do little in the way of formal drill and practice. At first their spoken utterances are very brief, and deviant from adult norms; but motivated as they are to understand, to be understood, and to get their own way, they rapidly master the system of language rules which will allow them to produce their own original messages. Perhaps, it began to be thought, second language learners could show similar motivation and success if they too were encouraged to concern themselves with meaning rather than with matters of form.

It was another applied linguist, Pit Corder, who drew language teachers' attention to the fact that foreign language learners already resemble L1 learners in some respects – notably in the pattern of errors that they make. Audio-lingual theorists of the 1950s had tried to persuade teachers that all learner errors must be rigorously corrected, for fear of fossilisation. Corder and others argued, however, that errors too were 'natural' – an inevitable feature of a learner's progress from a primitive version of the target language to a more elaborated version, and indeed, welcome evidence of the learner's stage of development. They questioned the need for rigorous correction, arguing that over time, FL learners' errors would correct themselves, as L1 learners' do.

A final contribution to the mix of ideas was a sceptical attack, most popularly expressed by the psycholinguist Stephen Krashen (1981), on the usefulness of grammar explanation and language analysis more generally. Krashen argued that under pressure of real-time language use, conscious grammatical knowledge is simply unavailable to improve performance and can never contribute to the development of target language fluency. While this view is not universally shared, weaker forms of this argument have led to a questioning of the traditional place of grammar teaching at the centre of classroom learning.

Against this background, there have been extended debates on the mix of classroom activities which would add up to a recognisable communicative methodology. While many different views have been expressed, most commentators would agree on the following:

1 Classroom activities should maximise opportunities for learners to use the target language for meaningful purposes, with their attention on the messages they are creating and the task they are completing, rather than on correctness of language form and language structure;
2 Learners trying their best to use the target language creatively and unpredictably are bound to make errors; this is a normal part of language learning, and constant correction is unnecessary, and even counterproductive;
3 Language analysis and grammar explanation may help some learners, but extensive experience of target language use helps everyone!

From these general ideas follow many current practices in the communicative classroom, especially the emphasis on creative role plays, projects, surveys, and other tasks and activities relevant to learners' interests, with unpredictable (and sometimes behavioural) outcomes. A 'communicative' practitioner is likely to make regular and systematic use of such activities at the heart of his or her scheme of work, not relegate them to the status of occasional special events.

From these ideas also follows the renewed emphasis (evident for example in programmes of study for the national curriculum for Modern Foreign Languages) on using the target language as the normal medium of classroom communication. Children are thoroughly familiar with the everyday routines of the classroom; the communicative practitioner exploits this fact, knowing that he or she can use this prior knowledge, as well as gestures and objects in the immediate environment, to ensure that messages about classroom organisation and activity instructions are understood. What is more, even where messages are not immediately understood, the communicative practitioner does not panic, but exploits the 'problem' as a further opportunity for target language use (for example, building up familiarity with ways of expressing, 'What did you say? Could you repeat, please? Sorry, I haven't understood'). And so, it is believed, the communicative practitioner is equipping learners with the 'coping strategies' they will need in the longer term, if they are to stay afloat in more and more extended and open-ended target language interaction.

Linked with this first group of principles, which are grounded in specific debates about language learning theory, are a second group, which reinforce and support the first, but have their origins in more general educational debates about learning and teaching:

4 Effective language teaching is responsive to the needs and interests of the individual learner;
5 Effective language learning is an active process, in which the learner takes increasing responsibility for his or her progress;
6 The effective teacher aims to facilitate, not control, the language learning process.

It is this second group of principles which may lead the communicative practitioner, at times, to negotiate the content of classroom tasks and activities with the pupils; to promote pair, group and individual activities; to introduce discussion and reflection on the language learning process itself and the language learning strategies being used by the pupils (if necessary, in L1); and to encourage self-assessment. More specifically, this group of principles may lead the communicative practitioner to reassess the role in language learning of the receptive skills, especially reading (currently marginalised in many classrooms where a 'communicative approach' is interpreted as essentially an oral approach). Schemes of work which systematically promote pupils' confidence and skill in extensive target language reading, via book boxes, graded reading schemes, reading diaries, etc., are clearly a contribution to producing more independent and self-motivated learners.

And what of materials? Diversity and, especially, authenticity have been key concerns for the communicative approach. By 'authentic' is commonly meant the use of materials originally produced for a native speaker audience – for example, media programmes, magazines, newspapers or recordings of spontaneous conversation. It has been argued that such materials have high credibility with language learners, who can appreciate their origins in the 'real world' outside the classroom. It has also been argued that such materials accustom learners to processing the kind of language they will themselves meet in real world situations, with all its messy spontaneity. (Compare the features of an unscripted conversation with a scripted dialogue which is read aloud!)

However, it has also been pointed out that any materials are only as 'authentic' as the use which is made of them, and the ways in which learners engage with them. Even in the real world, we adapt our language use sensitively to take account of the abilities of the person we are talking to – we do not talk to little children in the same way as to an educated adult, for example. So, a clear constraint on the original notion of 'authenticity' is the view that classroom materials should be relevant and accessible to their language learner audience. In practice, most communicative classrooms use a mix of materials, some 'authentic' in this first sense, others adapted or specially devised for a language learner audience, but typically modelled on 'real world' speech events and language genres.

PROBLEMS AND FUTURE DIRECTIONS

The impact of the 'communicative approach' on language teaching and learning has been enormous, and has led to increasing confidence on the part of classroom teachers that they can provide positive, worthwhile and attainable objectives for most learners, and make the classroom learning process varied and enjoyable.

At the same time, a variety of tensions and problems remain, which mean that change in classroom practices will be a continuing process for the foreseeable future.

The most obvious 'problem issue' is the question of grammar. It is clear that in some contexts, versions of the 'communicative approach' are producing learners who can still do little more than reproduce unanalysed global phrases, and have not yet internalised a creative language system (i.e. a grammar), which will allow them to produce original utterances correctly in situations of open and unpredictable target language use. As 'A' level foreign language teachers are very aware, the British GCSE examination is not free from this problem.

Theorists of communicative language teaching have long recognised this issue, and suggested pragmatic solutions; Christopher Brumfit (1985), for example, has advocated that teachers should plan systematically for a balance between meaning-oriented 'fluency' work and form-oriented 'accuracy' work, and many classroom practitioners have undoubtedly continued to teach grammar more or less systematically in traditional ways, alongside more innovative practices. However, at present we lack any developed understanding of the most effective and principled way to tackle grammar instruction as a component of an approach which remains communicative overall, and research and discussion will certainly focus on this question in coming years.

A second 'problem' concerns the relationship between doing on the one hand, and reflecting on the other. The communicative approach has advocated high levels of learner activity and involvement in target language use for 'real' communicative purposes; teachers have been urged, most obviously, to speak the target language at all times, and to minimise explanations. On the other hand, the concern to develop learner autonomy implies adoption of a more reflective approach to learning. This is seen in the current interest in promoting learners' conscious awareness of their own learning strategies, already mentioned above; it is difficult to see how extended discussion on such strategies could take place without use of the mother tongue.

Finally, as we have also seen, the 'communicative approach' has been interpreted to date, at least in British schools, as very largely an oral approach. The skills of reading and writing have so far been marginalised, rather than re-thought, as components of the overall approach. There are hopeful new local developments here, and the national curriculum framework may also offer an opportunity for more general rethinking of foreign language literacy skills, both as communicative goals in their own right and as tools for language learning. But again, much remains to be done.

CONCLUSION

This chapter has tried to show that the 'communicative approach' to language teaching is a fluid and changing body of ideas, not a fixed package. At present, none the less, many language educators like the label, which they feel expresses something significant both about their objectives and the way in which they choose to teach. As the approach matures we become more conscious of its limitations, and identify issues in our current practice which require debate and experimentation. A teaching profession which truly values its professionalism will involve new and experienced teachers alike in this ongoing process.

REFERENCES

Austin, J.L. (1962) *How to Do Things with Words*, Milton Keynes: Open University Press.
Breen, M.P. (1987) 'Contemporary paradigms in syllabus design. Parts 1 and 2', *Language Teaching* 20(2): 81–92; 20(3): 157–74.
Brumfit, C.J. (1985) *Language and Literature Teaching: From Practice to Principle*, Oxford: Pergamon.
Canale, M. (1983) 'From communicative competence to communicative language pedagogy', in J. Richards and R. Schmidt (eds) *Language and Communication*, Harlow: Longman.

Corder, S.P. (1981) *Error Analysis and Interlanguage*, Oxford: Oxford University Press.

Harding, A., Page, B. and Rowell, S. (eds) (1980) *Graded Objectives in Modern Languages*, London: Centre for Information on Language Teaching and Research (CILT).

Hymes, D. (1972) 'On communicative competence', in J. Pride and J. Holmes (eds) *Sociolinguistics*, Harmondsworth: Penguin.

Krashen, S.J. (1981) *Second Language Acquisition and Second Language Learning*, Oxford: Pergamon.

Littlewood, W. (1981) *Communicative Language Teaching*, Cambridge: Cambridge University Press.

Van Ek, J. (1975) *The Threshold Level*, Strasbourg: Council of Europe.

Wilkins, D.A. (1972) *Notional Syllabuses*, Oxford: Oxford University Press.

Chapter 4

The communicative approach and authentic texts

David Little, Seán Devitt and David Singleton

The purpose of this chapter is to summarise the principles that underpin the communicative approach in general and the use of authentic texts as a main source of target language input in particular. Although the communicative approach did not arise directly from language acquisition research, we shall see that in its fundamentals it coincides closely with the findings of that research. We shall also see that the increasingly central role that authentic texts have come to occupy in communicative language teaching methodology can be justified as much in terms of language acquisition research findings as in terms of basic communicative principles.

COMMUNICATIVE PRINCIPLES

The communicative approach to language teaching derives its name and its essential character from the fact that at every stage – the setting of learning targets, the definition of a syllabus, the development of learning materials, the elaboration and implementation of classroom activities, and the assessment of learners' progress – it focuses on language as a medium of communication. In this it differs from the traditions in language teaching that it seeks to replace. Both the grammar-translation and the audio-lingual/audio-visual methods focus from first to last on the grammatical system of the target language (no doubt both methods would claim to be teaching languages for communication, but that is a different matter). The communicative methodologies that have emerged over the past decade and a half have insisted with increasing confidence on the importance of engaging learners in activities which require them to communicate in the target language. By promoting learning not just *for* but *through* communication the communicative approach aligns itself with one of the basic facts of 'naturalistic' language acquisition.

In its most rigorous form, perhaps best exemplified by the 'threshold level' specifications and related documents produced by the Council of Europe's modern languages projects, the communicative approach never loses sight of the fact that all communication takes place in a physical setting and between participants, and has a social purpose. The typical communicative syllabus begins by considering who its learners are in terms of such characteristics as age, educational background, and previous language learning experience. It then goes on to define the needs that the learners will satisfy by learning the target language, including the communicative purposes that competence in the language will enable them to fulfil. This makes it possible to describe in some detail the kinds of language behaviour that successful learners should be capable of at the end of their course of learning. Thus the learner-centredness of the communicative approach arises directly from an analysis of the social functions of language.

Probably the two most widespread misconceptions about the communicative approach are (i) that it is concerned exclusively with the spoken language, and (ii) that it is indifferent to grammar. The first misconception probably arose because the earliest communicative projects were concerned with learners whose principal need was for a basic competence in oral communication. The Council of Europe's 'threshold level' specifications were originally designed to fulfil the needs of migrant workers; and the Graded Objectives movement in the United Kingdom was conceived as a way of bringing foreign language learning within the realistic reach of pupils of lower ability. But it is obvious that in literate societies written language performs a multitude of communicative purposes, so that reading and writing can be as important as listening and speaking in some communicative curricula. (At the same time, because the methods of western education depend so thoroughly on literacy skills, it is easy for teachers to overlook the fact that the great majority of people, including some of the most highly educated, make relatively little use of the writing skill in their daily life once full-time education is behind them.)

The belief that the communicative approach is indifferent to grammar seems to take two forms. On the one hand there are those who believe that it is hostile to the explicit treatment of grammar as a matter of pedagogical principle. This is not so; indeed, the earliest communicative documents emphasised the need for an eclectic methodology rather than one conforming to any particular orthodoxy. On the other hand there are those who maintain that because the communicative approach is above all interested in exchanges of meaning, it fails to give grammatical form its due. There are two answers to this argument. First, in all languages form and meaning are closely interrelated. It is true that we often succeed in communicating our intended meanings despite formal inadequacies of one kind or another – this frequently happens to all of us not only in foreign languages but also in our first language. However, there is a point beyond which disregard of grammatical form virtually guarantees a breakdown in communication. In a very real sense communication depends on grammar. Second, although much communicative methodology gives meaning priority over form, this merely emphasises the importance of exploring formal issues within a meaningful context; it does not amount to a disregard of grammar. On the contrary, because meaning and form are closely interrelated, a central part of the communicative purpose is to discover means of enabling learners to understand more acutely how the forms of their target language are organised in the creation of meaning.

AUTHENTIC TEXTS AND THE COMMUNICATIVE APPROACH

From the beginning 'authenticity' has been one of the key concepts of the communicative movement in language teaching. After all, if we are primarily concerned with language as a medium of communication, we shall want to ensure that there is a strong thread of continuity between what goes on in our classrooms and the characteristic modes of communication in our target language community. A major problem with language teaching methodologies that are centred on the target language system is precisely that they all too easily leave the learner without secure bridges into the actual world of language use. If its claims are to have any validity, the communicative approach must foster actual communication through the target language in the classroom; for only then can we be sure that our learners are able to communicate through the language. Again we are forcibly reminded of the fact that 'naturalistic' language acquisition occurs *through* communication.

Any course of learning involves four obligatory factors: a learner, a goal, content and a process. The communicative approach is concerned to observe the principle of authenticity in regard to each of them. In other words, it is concerned that in every dimension the course of learning should be appropriate to the learner's needs, expectations and experience on the one hand and to the realities of communication in the target language community on the other.

Essentially an authentic text is a text that was created to fulfil some social purpose in the language community in which it was produced. Thus novels, poems, newspaper and magazine articles, handbooks and manuals, recipes, and telephone directories are all examples of authentic texts; and so too are radio and television broadcasts and computer programmes. As far as language teaching is concerned, however, 'authentic text' has come to have a rather more limited meaning than this. Many attempts to implement the communicative approach have found no use for literary texts (sometimes this is entirely appropriate to the learners' needs, but often it reflects a prejudice against the study of literary texts as a hangover from the grammar-translation method); and even in the last quarter of the twentieth century the physical reality of most classrooms prohibits the frequent use of video or computer materials. Accordingly, when language teachers use the term 'authentic text' they often mean a piece of writing that originally appeared in a newspaper or magazine and is probably of ephemeral value and interest.

Most language coursebooks published in the past decade have contained their share of authentic texts in this sense of the term. The problem is, of course, that such texts are usually out of date before the coursebook is published.

There are essentially three reasons why well-chosen authentic texts should occupy a central role in any second language learning process. First, because they have been written for a communicative purpose they are more interesting than texts which have been invented to illustrate the usage of some feature of the target language; learners are thus likely to find them more motivating than invented texts. Second, because they revolve around content rather than form, authentic texts are more likely to have acquisition-promoting content than invented texts. This is partly because they provide a richer linguistic diet, and partly because they encourage learners to concentrate on penetrating to the meaning that lies beneath the surface structures. Third, if used in sufficient quantities authentic texts can begin to replicate the 'language bath' in which the first language learner is immersed from birth. Clearly, the child learning its first language or the adult immersed in a second language community enjoys an infinitely higher level of exposure to the target language than can easily be provided by a language classroom at some distance from the target language community. Of course, the teacher can begin to replicate the conditions of 'naturalistic' acquisition by using the target language as the normal medium of classroom management and instruction. But a large and varied diet of authentic texts is essential if the teacher is to create a genuinely acquisition-rich environment. In the foreign language classroom authentic texts can serve as a partial substitute for the community of native speakers within which 'naturalistic' language acquisition occurs; the more authentic texts we confront our learners with, the more opportunities we shall create for acquisition to take place. Once again the findings of language acquisition research support common-sense intuitions.

Children typically acquire the forms of their mother tongue *after* they have learned how to participate in highly organised interaction. We might expand the point by saying that they first master the 'vertical' structures of discourse, and that this provides them with the framework within which they master the 'horizontal' structures of syntax and morphology. Thus they acquire language in the very process of using it as a more or less efficient medium of communication: mastery of 'horizontal' structures arises from constant practice in the communication of meaning within 'vertical' structures. The use of authentic texts as the chief source of target language input allows the second language learner to follow a similar course of development.

Comprehension is an essential component of communication, and thus a precondition for efficient language acquisition. It requires access to three kinds of knowledge. First, we need to be able to draw on knowledge of the world, the ever-increasing stock of facts and hypotheses that we accumulate from the business of attentive living. This enables us to fix our general bearings and provides us with what might be described as a 'plausibility filter': the meanings that we attach to utterances and texts do not conflict with our world knowledge. Second, we need to be able to draw on knowledge of the norms of discourse. This knowledge tells us what kind of communicative event we are involved in and helps us to generate appropriate expectations of its structure and outcome. Third, we need to be able to draw on our gradually developing linguistic knowledge, that is, our knowledge of the grammar of the language in question.

It is often assumed that authentic texts are more difficult for language learners to cope with than invented texts. If coping is a matter of word-for-word translation, this may well be the case. But the comprehension on which effective language acquisition depends is not a matter of word-for-word translation – the child learning its first language cannot, after all, use translation as an aid to learning. It is our contention that if they are properly handled, authentic texts promote acquisition because they challenge learners to activate relevant knowledge of the world, of discourse and of the language system, and thus construct the conditions for further learning. The essential point is that authentic texts appropriate to a particular group of learners will belong to text types and deal with topics with which those learners are already more or less familiar. Clearly, they will need to be provided with various aids to comprehension, but they themselves will be able to contribute much in the way of understanding by drawing on their existing knowledge.

What we have said about authentic texts in relation to language acquisition processes reaffirms the communicative principle that meaning has priority over form. The argument of the preceding paragraphs assumes that authentic texts should be used authentically: that their exploitation in the classroom should be shaped by a general awareness that they were written for a particular communicative purpose. At the same time, however, we must not overlook the fact that native speakers sometimes focus on form, using their knowledge of the grammar of their mother tongue in order to understand structurally complex passages, or reading authentic texts with a view to enhancing their competence in their mother tongue. In the same way authentic texts provide a living context for the treatment of grammar for foreign learners.

Chapter 5

De l'imparfait du subjonctif aux méthodes communicatives
Où en est l'enseignement des langues vivantes?

Francis Debyser

L'enseignement du français langue étrangère a fait des progrès considérables depuis trente ans; ces progrès portent aussi bien sur la conception des programmes que sur les instruments méthodologiques, manuels et méthodes, sur les techniques de classe et d'animation, sur les procédures d'évaluation et sur ce qui est peut-être le plus important, la formation et le professionnalisme des enseignants.

Tous ces aspects de la pédagogie des langues étrangères sont si étroitement liés qu'ils sont interdépendants; ils constituent le domaine de ce qu'on appelle aujourd'hui la *didactique des langues*, discipline constituée et reconnue aussi bien dans les établissements de formation de professeurs que dans les programmes universitaires de tous les pays. Si cette discipline a été reconnue et légitimée ce n'est pas uniquement à cause de sa spécificité ou du caractère scientifique de ses démarches et de ses méthodes de recherche, mais en raison de son utilité; de même que la médecine ne se confond pas avec la biologie mais sert à guérir les malades, de même la didactique des langues ne se confond pas avec la linguistique mais sert à enseigner les langues vivantes; la didactique des langues n'a, en effet, obtenu cette reconnaissance universitaire et scientifique que parce qu'elle fonde une pratique pédagogique plus rationnelle et plus efficace, et peut donc mieux répondre aux attentes, aux besoins et aux motivations des élèves, au souci d'efficacité des professeurs, aux objectifs des systèmes éducatifs et aux intérêts des sociétés; une pratique plus rationnelle parce que fondée sur les sciences du langage, de la communication et de l'éducation; une pratique plus efficace parce que plus fonctionelle, plus pragmatique et plus concrète.

La cohérence de la didactique des langues, sa rationalité et son efficacité se trouvent aujourd'hui représentées par les propositions méthodologiques pour l'enseignement des langues vivantes connues sous le nom d'approches ou de méthodes *communicatives*.

Ce sont les principes de ces approches et de ces méthodes que nous nous proposons de définir à grands traits, avec le souci de montrer qu'il ne s'agit pas d'une mode, ni d'une rupture brutale avec les acquis, les progrès et l'experience du passé, ni d'un engouement théorique de spécialistes, ni d'une opération publicitaire ou commerciale mais de l'état actuel des progrès de la didactique des langues. Il ne faut pas non plus y voir un aboutissement définitif: la didactique des langues n'est ni arrêtée, ni accomplie, ni parfaite; elle doit encore évoluer et a d'autres progrès à faire comme les autres sciences et disciplines humaines.

APPRENDRE À COMMUNIQUER: UNE HISTOIRE EN DEUX ÉTAPES

Certains termes nouveaux sont inutilement obscurs, celui de méthode communicative ne l'est pas, il est au contraire transparent et doit être pris à la lettre; une méthode communicative est une méthode qui enseigne, qui permet d'apprendre à communiquer en langue étrangère.

On peut même se dire que le terme est si transparent, si évident qu'il est banal et n'apporte rien de nouveau. Ce n'est pas vrai: on s'en aperçoit quand on regarde d'un peu plus près l'évolution des méthodes de langues vivantes dans les systèmes scolaires et universitaires où l'on peut distinguer deux grandes étapes antérieures.

Apprendre des formes et des règles

L'enseignement traditionnel des langues était autrefois fondé sur l'apprentissage des formes et des règles. Le but n'était pas d'apprendre à communiquer mais d'apprendre la grammaire des langues étudiées; objectif dont on n'est pas sûr qu'il soit nécessaire et dont on sait qu'il n'est pas suffisant pour apprendre à communiquer de façon élémentaire, par exemple pour demander un renseignement ou un conseil, pour échanger oralement ou par écrit des informations simples, ou même se présenter à quelqu'un, saluer un visiteur; c'est l'exemple tant de fois cité de l'élève qui a étudié une langue pendant six ans et qui, se trouvant à l'étranger, n'est pas capable de demander son chemin dans la rue ni de téléphoner pour prendre un rendez-vous. Seuls parvenaient à échapper à cet échec de la communication les élèves qui avaient été exposés à des méthodes directes, plus actives et qui comportaient déjà certains aspects communicatifs comme, par exemple, le fait de n'utiliser dans la classe que la langue étudiée.

D'autres élèves parvenaient à communiquer malgré tout, ceux auxquels la chance ou la fortune permettaient de séjourner à l'étranger ou de pratiquer réellement la langue dont ils n'avaient étudié que la grammaire.

Imiter les échanges

La première référence explicite à la communication a été faite par la linguistique moderne qui définit précisément les langues comme des systèmes de signes permettant de communiquer. On comprend donc que les premières méthodes inspirées de la linguistique appliquée, notamment les méthodes structurales et les méthodes audiovisuelles, aient donné une place plus grande à la communication. Cela s'est traduit par un grand progrès dans l'enseignement des langues vivantes. On a cessé d'enseigner des formes et des règles dans le vide ou appliquées à des exemples et à des phrases isolées, et on a vu apparaître des méthodes où les mots et les constructions les plus fréquentes, les plus usuelles et, croyait-on, les plus utiles à la communication, étaient présentés non pas isolément mais dans des contextes, des situations et des dialogues imitant des échanges communicatifs conversationnels.

Ces méthodes ont en général tenu leurs promesses dans des cours intensifs dotés de conditions et d'équipements modernes destinés à des groupes restreints d'élèves motivés, notamment d'adultes. Ils ont eu moins d'efficacité qu'on ne l'espérait lorsque ces conditions n'étaient pas réunies: cours extensifs d'une ou deux périodes par semaine, absence d'équipements audiovisuels, classes trop nombreuses, élèves médiocrement motivés, professeurs insuffisamment formés. La déception a été parfois d'autant plus grande que les éducateurs attendaient une amélioration qualitative spectaculaire des résultats au moment même où le développement scolaire et la démocratisation de l'instruction, phénomène mondial commun aux pays industrialisés et aux pays en voie de développement, attiraient massivement vers les établissements scolaires, et donc vers l'enseignement des langues étrangères, des populations d'élèves souvent dix fois plus nombreuses. On oublie presque toujours cet aspect lorsqu'on compare les résultats actuels à ceux d'autrefois.

MÉTHODES COMMUNICATIVES: QUATRE ORIENTATIONS

Quoi qu'il en soit, un bilan critique des méthodes dites structurales s'imposait que l'on pourrait commencer par une question simple (même si la réponse l'est moins): pourquoi des méthodes conversationnelles faisant une place importante à l'oral, au dialogue et à la langue contemporaine, pour ne pas dire la langue de tous les jours, c'est-à-dire à des aspects essentiels de la communication négligés dans les méthodes antérieures, ne permettaient pas de donner à coup sûr aux élèves la compétence de communication?

Cela nous permettra d'indiquer en même temps les principales orientations des méthodes communicatives. Cet examen critique n'a pas pour but de faire un procès stérile et injuste aux méthodes structurales; certains outils font leurs preuves et rendent des services pendant une période donnée; le moment arrive un jour cependant où il faut les adapter ou les remplacer. Il s'agit surtout d'examiner les points à améliorer pour réaliser d'autres instruments méthodologiques visant plus directement à l'apprentissage de la communication en langue étrangère. De ce point de vue quatre points faibles des méthodes structurales ou audiovisuelles ont été relevés.

Un retour au sens

Les méthodes structurales s'étaient directement inspirées des recherches linguistiques prédominantes à l'époque et qui étaient caractérisées par un excès de formalisme. La linguistique formelle vise à une description scientifique d'une langue, d'un code ou d'un système de signes en limitant au maximum le recours au sens; ou, pour dire les choses plus simplement, la linguistique formelle s'intéresse davantage à la structure du language qu'aux significations qu'il véhicule. Mais ce qui est une option méthodologique de recherche légitime pour un théoricien est vite devenu une erreur pédagogique.

En effet, l'élève qui apprend une langue étrangère n'a pas les mêmes préoccupations que le linguiste; la seule chose qui compte pour lui c'est le sens, soit qu'il essaie de s'exprimer: dans ce cas ce qui lui importe est de communiquer du sens avec des formes nouvelles; soit qu'il cherche à comprendre et dans ce cas il cherche à tirer du sens d'une suite de formes étrangères. Or, trop souvent les méthodes struturales ou audiovisuelles ont fait le contraire; comme si le but était de faire acquérir en priorité les structures de la langue étrangère à l'élève en espérant qu'ensuite il pourrait les utiliser en les chargeant de sens. Le retour à la grammaire du sens, à une pédagogie de la signification s'est imposé progressivement; ce retour à la sémantique inverse la priorité formes-sens, pour le reproposer dans un ordre plus naturel sens-formes qu'illustrait si bien au début du siècle l'ouvrage fondamental de Ferdinand Brunot *La pensée et la langue*. Les formes de la langue sont au service de l'organisation, de l'expression et de la pensée, afin de pouvoir communiquer. La connaissance des formes et des structures reste indispensable en langue étrangère, mais elle est toujours au service d'un projet de sens, d'expression, de communication.

Les méthodes communicatives marquent un retour à la grammaire notionnelle, grammaire des notions, des idées et de l'organisation du sens et les progressions qu'elles proposent, au lieu d'être des progressions formelles, sont des progressions plus souples permettant à l'élève avant toute chose de produire et de comprendre du sens.

Une pédagogie moins répétitive

Les méthodes structurales et audiovisuelles insistaient beaucoup sur la répétition, le conditionnement structural, l'apprentissage intensif de «mécanismes», et parlaient même d'«automatismes». Cela avait pour conséquence que malgré les dialogues qui constituaient le point de départ des leçons, la plus grande partie du temps de travail des élèves en classe était consacrée à des répétitions ou à des réemplois mécaniques. On justifiait d'ailleurs cette pédagogie en se référant à des théories de l'apprentissage par conditionnement aujourd'hui à peu près unanimement récusées. Cela aboutissait parfois à des pratiques de classe, surtout lorsque le professeur manquait d'expérience, rigides, répétitives, monotones et n'ayant que peu de rapports avec la communication réelle. Les méthodes communicatives ont remis à une place plus raisonnable les exercices formels et répétitifs pour développer dans les classes des exercices de communication réelle ou simulée beaucoup plus interactifs conformément à une hypothèse de bon sens qui est que c'est en communiquant qu'on apprend à communiquer.

La centration sur l'apprenant

Cette formule plutôt pédante signifie qu'en pédagogie, l'élève est plus important que la méthode. L'élève est le sujet et l'acteur principal de l'apprentissage et non son objet ou le simple destinataire d'une méthode. Cette orientation concerne la pédagogie générale; si on l'applique à la didactique des langues, surtout si cette didactique a pour objectif la compétence de communication, les conséquences méthodologiques sont importantes.

Pour communiquer l'élève ne se contentera pas d'énoncér des phrases grammaticales dans le vide mais des énoncés dont il sera le sujet actif et impliqué; il recevra également des messages dont il sera le destinataire réel. Les méthodes communicatives doivent logiquement et nécessairement le préparer à cela et proposer des leçons, des exercices et des pratiques de classes où les références au passé, au présent, à l'avenir, à l'espace, aux interlocuteurs s'organisent comme dans la communication réelle. L'élève doit aussi pouvoir maîtriser, nuancer, modaliser son expression, être capable d'insister ou au contraire de marquer des distances, de poser un fait comme certain, comme possible, simplement probable, faisant problème, etc. On comprend tout de suite l'importance de ces aspects dans les échanges.

Les approches communicatives ont fait des efforts remarquables pour introduire ces éléments dans l'apprentissage des langues, aidées en cela par des recherches récentes de la linguistique qui ne se limite plus à l'étude de la phrase et du système de la langue mais s'intéresse de plus en plus au fonctionnement du discours, à la grammaire de la parole, de l'énonciation, des textes.

Aspects sociaux et pragmatiques de la communication

Les méthodes traditionelles faisaient apprendre des phrases artificielles: la mer est bleue, Paul a un joli vélo, la robe de ma mère est verte . . .

Les méthodes audiovisuelles ou structurales ont modernisé le matériel linguistique d'apprentissage mais sont restées en deçà de la communication réelle où les énoncés ont toujours un enjeu; on utilise le langage pour se présenter, s'excuser, demander, permettre, exprimer une opinion, accepter, refuser, etc.

Les méthodes communicatives prennent directement ces performances communicatives: être capable de se présenter, etc., comme objectifs de leçon. On n'enseigne pas la forme interrogative comme objet en soi, on enseigne à demander une information. On n'enseigne pas l'impératif comme forme mais on enseigne à demander à quelqu'un de faire quelque chose, ce qui demande des moyens linguistiques qui ne se réduisent pas à l'impératif très souvent exclu pour des raisons de courtoisie. La méthodologie audiovisuelle ne s'était pas préoccupée de cet aspect pragmatique de la communication faisant l'hypothèse qu'une fois qu'on connaît les bases d'une langue étrangère on est capable de faire tout cela. Les approches communicatives leur ont au contraire donné une importance de première place en suivant les recommandations du Conseil de l'Europe pour l'enseignement de l'anglais, du français et de l'allemand.

Réorienter la méthodologie en ce sens n'est pas sans poser de problèmes:

– l'un est de ne pas bouleverser complètement la méthodologie et de conserver dans l'enseignement en milieu scolaire une certaine régularité de la progression linguistique et une importance plus grande qu'on n'a tendance à le faire à la systématisation des acquisitions linguistiques.
– un autre est d'adapter ce type d'approche aux besoins, aux motivations et aux habitudes d'apprentissage de publics particuliers.

Un troisième point est de mieux mettre en évidence les spécificités culturelles des apprenants si l'on veut que la communication sociale respecte les règles culturelles auxquelles elle obéit dans la langue de l'élève ou tout au moins en tienne compte.

Le quatrième problème, le plus important, est que ces nouvelles orientations soient discutées et appropriées par les enseignants. Plus dynamiques et plus motivantes elles peuvent éventuellement déconcerter les professeurs; il convient évidemment de les y préparer et non de les leur imposer.

Chapter 6

Communication
Sense and nonsense

Michael Grenfell

A spectre is haunting language teaching – Communication! Surely this must be a facile remark. Is it not true that every modern coursebook, resource pack and syllabus is devoutly communicative? There must be hundreds. Applied Linguistic research too has supplied ample evidence for the view that communication is 'the' key to an effective teaching methodology. With this amount of support it would be perhaps unsurprising to report success in learning languages of hitherto unknown proportions. Yet this is clearly not the case. I am not wishing to be a pessimist, but, despite the energy and enthusiasm in all things language learning at the moment, a successful method seems rather more a statement of intent than practice. Why is this so? All that glisters, it appears, is not gold. Our National Syllabus – GCSE – turns out to be a transactional wolf in a communicative sheep's clothing. Coursebooks once heralded as the new generation now seem, after years of teaching with them, not to be so interactive after all. Why is this the case? And why, if communication is so effective as a means of learning languages, is it so elusive? In this chapter, I want to set out a brief summary of how, in methodological terms, we have arrived at the stage we are now at and try to suggest why present practice is often not as effective as we would wish. I then want to attempt to reorientate our perspective and lay down certain key principles in founding a new approach to method.

Method and methodology are themselves problematic terms. As I understand them, they imply a clear set of guidelines, or a series of sequences to follow. So, for example, Pattern Practice or the Direct Method was a methodology. Its obvious attractiveness arose from the way it seemingly combined the recognised need to 'know' grammar with the intent to 'use' language actively in 'communicative' contexts. There was a neatness about its practice that was (is?) extremely seductive. First, language had to be contextualised. No argument there. For too long, textbooks had presented language in *ad hoc*, multifarious situations. Any connecting sense in these was often remote; the major objective being instead to highlight particular syntactic features. Second, lessons proceeded along the precise sequence of Presentation, Practice and Production. The assumption behind this was reasonable enough: before learners can do anything with the language there had to be input, and it is only when language has been reworked and partly digested that pupils are 'free' to produce language in any generative sense. Third, the teacher had another powerful weapon in his or her arsenal – three-stage questioning. Equipped with a good set of flashcards or OHP foils, and after lots of initial repetition exercises, a typical sequence would run as follows:

Stage 1   *Il va au cinéma. Oui ou non?*
    2   *Il va au cinéma ou il va au café?*
    3   *Où va-t-il?*

Here, the withdrawal and thus level of support given to pupils is implicit in the demands of the questions themselves. Indeed, the ability to gauge language so as to elicit particular pupil responses is helpful in the course of any lesson.

The Direct Method is therefore just that – a method. Why then, despite its attractions, has it been superseded? One reason is that a lot of the language taught in such a way is often too impersonal, too involved with other people doing other things, too third rather than first person based. Moreover, structural/grammar points remain the core of such work. Everything else stems from them. Furthermore, although the language work is contextualised, these contexts themselves are often rather con-trived – I have yet to see a convincing situation for a direct method approach to teaching preceding direct object pronouns in French! Finally, the atmosphere of such lessons is highly interrogative. By being based around questions and answers, the teacher can become a sort of interroga-tor, relentlessly questioning pupils in the belief that it is only by reaching the third 'production' stage of the lesson that he or she can be sure that the particular language point has been learnt. Yet, for all the talk of assimilation and productive language, there is real doubt that learners are indeed acquiring active usage of the language in any real sense, outside of a lot of carefully constructed contexts. Language acquisition which does occur seems to take place 'elsewhere'. Of course, with the most gifted teachers the Direct Method becomes a whole lot more, but these indi-viduals appear to possess qualities which make a success of any method or approach.

The new-style communicative techniques attached themselves to the Direct Method in a seemingly natural way; so much so that it is often difficult to spot the joins where one becomes the other and vice versa. And yet the change in perspective is quite radical. For a start we no longer have a method so much as an approach;[1] no longer specific stages and sequences but a set of guiding principles. The neatest summary of these lists ten key phrases:

1 Intention to mean	6 Target language use
2 Information gap	7 Approach to error
3 Personalisation	8 Authenticity
4 Unpredictability	9 Speech v. writing
5 Legitimacy	10 Practice v. real language[2]

Clearly these are helpful in qualifying aspects of discourse in teaching. But how do you design activities which incorporate them? Furthermore, it may well be that communicative learning contains these features, but does the sum of them make communication? It is easy to believe that if these features are present, then so is communication, but this is not necessarily the case. In short, what is communication? And is the whole greater than the sum of its parts? Even our understanding of each of these features gives rise to problems of definition and interpretation. I shall take two examples in order to illustrate the point I am making: Information Gap and Personalisation.

There is little doubt that a strong motivational factor in learning languages is the want or need to know something, either at a factual or effective level. However, it is one thing to recognise this and design activities where pupils are required to discover and pass on information, thoughts and feelings, and quite another to base a whole lot of classroom work on exchanges of information mostly cued from given sources. Here is an information gap exercise from a GCSE examination, although it is typical of role plays found in many textbooks.

> Your tasks:
> 1 To find out how much it costs to send a letter to England
> 2 To ask if it is cheaper to send a postcard
> 3 To ask where to send a parcel
> 4 To ask where there is a telephone
> 5 To say thank you and goodbye[3]

A conversation arising from such cues will indeed represent an achievement at a basic level, but the language used is never likely to be anything other than of a fairly routinised phrase-book style. In this case, the exam board recognises that for higher level grades something more is required. Thus, in order to elicit more sophisticated language, they suggest that in reply to (3), the examiner asks, '*Qu'est-ce que ça contient?*' and '*Ça vaut combien?*' Yet, of course, there is no parcel, so how is the candidate expected to know what it contains and what its value is? This is not so much a linguistic problem as one of imagination; not so much conveying sense as trying to make sense of what is going on in a situation highly removed from any personally known facts. Discourse between individuals is not being generated in the context of shared understandings, so much as imposed in an overly prescribed manner. I conclude, therefore, that it is misleading to assume that such exchanges of information represent communication and are hence pedagogically effective.

Similarly, it may well be justified to reason that learners learn language best when they are conveying personal sense, in short when they want to express themselves: but this is not to see first person language forms as an end in themselves. Hence:

First, practise these conversations . . .
    1. A. *Est-ce que tu aimes* le cinéma?
        B. *Oui, beaucoup, mais je préfère la télèvision.* etc.
Next, use the same basic conversations but change the words . . .
    le cinéma   la radio
    le sport   la T.V.
      etc.[4]

Such exercises take rehearsal to an extreme. Just as in pattern practice, it is unlikely that such drilling makes any real use of the natural motivational force inherent in expressing oneself in conversation; the will to be understood at that particular point in the discourse. Again, even when such exercises are satisfactorily performed, there is real reason to doubt that much of the language will be recalled and actively used when needed in speech. Real language use is just not that tidy. It may well be possible to elicit the correct 'performance' for examination purposes, but does it teach pupils to take on board language as a medium for their own expressions in the real world? My conclusion is that, yes, we learn best when we are personally involved but activities based on personalised topics are not necessarily sufficient to do this; as the former implies an investment of concern that the latter can merely mimic. Yet a random review of current, popular, 'action based' coursebooks reveals that they are full of such exercises. The paradox is that the effect of the features of so-called communicative-based books is often depersonalising and uninvolving.

Many authors also apparently need to increase levels of difficulty in language in their coursebooks. Gradients of grammar may now be less common, but gradients of topically based notions and functions are not. Thus, the language of Book 2 is invariably more complex than Book 1 and 'easier' than Book 3. Yet it seems to me that it does not matter if you design language coursebooks around grammar, topics, or notions and functions, when the underlying principle is one of linear progression, the effect on the learner is to instil the sentiment that the teacher is always one step ahead of the pupil; and is thus always pushing, demanding a little bit more – more than the pupil wants to give. Pupils never have the satisfaction of consolidating, of moving off at a tangent to use, to explore, to play with the language on their own terms before moving on. The demands are rather on input and immediate output, with the teacher setting the pace. I am not arguing that there can be no progression, I am simply questioning how it is achieved. I often wonder how it is that a sizeable minority of pupils who begin their language learning with such fun and enthusiasm, finally, by the end of Year nine, seem so demotivated by apparent lack of success in it. They have no excitement for what languages have to offer them. I have concluded that it is often precisely because, and in apparent contradiction to, the practice of communicative techniques as we apply them. The time may be, therefore, ripe to reappraise these techniques; especially if they are going to form the basis of our work with pupils of all abilities in the new national curriculum.

I have claimed that many pupils do feel uninvolved when learning language, do not feel they are expressing themselves. The point is perhaps more profound than it may first appear. Research suggests that when we learn our first language, it is not only a way of getting things done, it is also an expression of sense of self. When Barnes[5] wrote of the importance of exploratory talk in the learning process, he stressed not only the moving of the learner into new areas of knowledge but the growth and development of the learner him- or herself in taking on board that knowledge; shaping and reshaping it as an expression of individual needs and as part of an empathetically shared world view. My conclusion from this, for our own sphere of language learning, is that it is not enough to take in the world that language represents. It is rather necessary to create oneself in and through that language. In other words, language is not something that we access like a baggage of information, taking out the bits and pieces to suit our needs at a particular instant. It is rather the means by which we create sense; of our world, of and for ourselves. In philosophical terms, it is the 'to be' rather than the 'to have' nature of language which characterises its use and growth. I believe that many learners do not share in this sense of being, in this sense of identity, in the predominant learning situations of many of our schools today.

Eric Hawkins,[6] in his 'How to do it' chapter of *Modern Languages in the Curriculum* states that languages are effectively learnt when pupils get things done in the language and have insight into structure. But there is a third vital component: a sense of self-identity in the language. The message of sociolinguistic and social psycholinguistic research literature is surely that language is the very blueprint of our identities as social beings. We need to express and explore this area in our social discourse, as it is only by doing this that language will expand; as a vehicle for identity and identities in interaction with each other. In order to do this, we need to *make* language as a creative act, open to all those features observed by applied linguists as support to this *act*; deviation, repair devices, elucidation, discourse dynamics, control strategies, etc., etc. I am therefore suggesting that communication does not so much arise from the totality of its features as spring from the energy that requires it to be. This is the spectre which haunts so much of language teaching methodology; and it is at once alluring and elusive. It is now the challenge of developers to design approaches, rather than materials, to shape such activity. Communication will not occur, therefore, by discovering the twenty-first use of a flashcard, or the thirty-first listening activity as the key to unlocking the communicative door. This is not to say that such activities are of little value. Indeed there will always be a place for lively materials presented in an imaginative way. But these will only partially succeed if teachers do not finally involve learners in a personal way, where they have a stake in what is created through language; in short, that they care.

Caring implies recognising value in language. Of course, the value of various learning activities has been implicit in language learning literature for some while. Hawkins[7] quotes Stevick in relating teaching activities to levels of personal meaning; phonetic practice, structural rehearsal, creative rehearsal and real performance. Heafford[8] expresses the same continuum more explicitly, and describes pupil activities in terms of low, mixed and high value. I would not disagree that 'high' level tasks – e.g. asking and answering questions, reading silently etc. – are more effective than 'low' level tasks – e.g. translating, reading aloud etc. – as they involve more sophisticated levels of conceptual thinking. Perhaps, however, it is more pertinent to go one stage further and suggest that it is not so much the value of activities which is so crucial as the value(s) of language itself. First, in the sense that language has the power to provoke responses and (all language in different ways) affect actions. Language needs to be seen by the learner as a potent tool in expression and reaction. It is a medium that can be shaped and moulded to individual needs and intentions. My response to learners who ask, 'Can I say . . .?' is 'Yes, you can say whatever you want – exciting isn't it?' There is time for correction and perfection. I regret that this sense of colour and contrast in language has been squeezed out of many topic-based coursebooks; children lose their sense of freedom in language. Second, and connected to this, is the value of individual components of language. Thus, I hope that individual learners become aware that some language buys them a lot in terms of what it will do for them; for example, 'je vais' is more useful than the verb 'tricoter'. There is, I suggest, a hierarchy of value within language itself aside from the pragmatics of topic work.

I have argued that it is the real lack of personal sense in many language courses today which is obscuring the true dynamic of language learning, that despite modern advances, we are still wedded to an overprescribed input and test approach in teaching languages. The comfortably tight structures this gives to schema, in fact, hinder the natural processes of language; in particular, the creative act that is communication. I keep faith with my spectre, but realise that it will only become flesh once we have broken the barriers of topic-based coursebooks in order to allow more freedom for personal identity to come forward. I am making a plea, therefore, for an organising principle; one which will adapt to the developmental strengths and needs of pupils at a particular stage of their language learning. We do not want or need more games and activities, but rather integrating techniques which will facilitate these processes.

NOTES

1 Richards, J.C. and Rodgers, T.S. 1986. *Approaches and Methods in Language Teaching: A description and analysis*. Cambridge: Cambridge University Press.
2 CILT: *Information Sheet No. 12*. 1989.
3 SEG: *GCSE Summer 1988 Paper 7*.
4 Honnor, S., Holt, R. and Taylor, H.M. 1980. *Tricolore 1*. Leeds: E.J. Arnold, p. 21.
5 Barnes, D. *et al*. 1969. *Language, the Learner and the School*. Harmondsworth: Penguin Books.
6 Hawkins, E. 1987. *Modern Languages in the Curriculum* (Revised). Cambridge: Cambridge University Press.
7 ibid., p. 256.
8 Heafford, M. March 1990. 'Teachers may teach, but do learners learn?', in *Language Learning Journal*, No. 1, p. 88.

Chapter 7

Mistakes are the mistake

Keith Morrow

Teachers of a foreign language seem to face two separate problems when it comes to mistakes their students make. The first is to recognise what constitutes a mistake. The second is the methodological problem of how to intervene; what remedial action can the teacher take to help the student to avoid the mistake in future. More crucially, perhaps, how can the teacher make the students recognise that a mistake has been made.

From the perspective of a teacher in the late eighties it may seem that communicative approaches to language teaching have had more to say about the first of these problems than the second. Indeed in this chapter I want to concentrate on this first question, but from the point of view of a language tester, basing what I have to say about what 'mistakes' are from work in developing a series of communicative tests of English as a foreign language. I then want to suggest that in fact 'mistakes' are not what is really important in evaluating and developing language performance.

WHAT IS A MISTAKE?

To the teachers of those of us brought up on a grammar-translation approach to foreign language learning, there would probably have seemed something fatuous about a question like this. Grammar was a question of rules; break the rules and you made a mistake. Circle the mistake in red pen. Get the miscreant to write out the correct version ten times. End of problem. Even if pupils had been encouraged to ask questions about why the mistake was a mistake (and they weren't!), the answer would have been simple:

> *ad* always takes the accusative. *Homo* is nominative. Therefore *ad homo* is wrong.
> *depuis* always takes the present tense. *J'ai habité* is the present perfect. Therefore *j'ai habité là depuis 1985* is wrong.

On that level, of course, the problem remains as clear-cut now as it was in the past. Nothing in the communicative approach turns ungrammatical utterances into grammatical ones, and the mistakes exemplified above would still seem rather peculiar to speakers of Latin or French. But on another level we are perhaps in a position now to take a rather more sophisticated view of what is going on. This sophistication lies in our interest in two further questions.

WHY ARE MISTAKES MADE?

One of the great developments associated with the communicative approach has been the concern of teachers and researchers not just with product (i.e. what learners actually produce or understand) but with process (i.e. what they have to do in order to produce or understand something). It is this concern with process which has been at the root of most of the interesting methodological developments associated with the communicative approach in recent years (for instance the use of information-gap activities).

In the 1970s studies of the process of language learning led Pit Corder[1] to propose that 'mistakes' made by learners of a foreign language are actually of two quite distinct sorts. The first, to which he gave the label *errors*, are caused by ignorance of the appropriate rule or structure in the foreign language. Essentially these are problems of knowledge, either of knowledge about some element of the language, or of knowledge how to use some language feature. The label *mistake* was given to a second and very different kind of problem. It may seem unhelpful to split hairs in this way and to suggest that two words which are accepted as synonyms in common usage can actually signify something essentially different. Yet the distinction between 'mistake' and 'error' is a crucial one which is highlighted by the more productive emphasis associated with the communicative approach.

A *mistake* for Pit Corder is a problem not of knowledge, but of application. Although you 'know' perfectly well that *depuis* is followed by the present tense, when you open your mouth to speak, it still comes out followed by the present perfect. This is a crucial problem for learners who wish to make use of their foreign language (for communication) rather than those who might have learnt it as an object of intellectual study in 'the old days'. The process of dredging up from your linguistic resources the right words in the right place to say what you mean is now seen as a vital part of learning to use a foreign language. When things go wrong with this process, the old traditions of the red pen and repetition may not have much to offer. In practice it may be very difficult to see whether a problem which a student is having is caused by lack of knowledge or inability to apply what she or he already 'knows'. But it behoves us to find out, because ways of helping with the problem will almost certainly be different in the two cases.[2]

DO MISTAKES MATTER?

This may seem at first a question as fatuous as the previous one. Of course mistakes matter. Well, yes and no. Mistakes may matter for two reasons. First, and perhaps surprisingly, they may be direct evidence for what the student 'knows' about the language system. The student of English who says *'Last night I taked my girlfriend to the cinema'* clearly knows that in general the past tense of verbs in English is formed with 'ed'. This will be very important information for the teacher concerned to build upon what the students know. Second, and less surprisingly, mistakes are equally direct evidence of problems the student is having. Whether he 'knows' that the past tense of this particular verb is irregular and has forgotten it in the heat of the moment, or whether he has never known it at all is a question the teacher may want to address.

'May' want to address, because on the other hand, mistakes may not matter. This heretical thought is perhaps the basis for the conviction among certain teachers that the communicative approach is somehow the soft option – that it allows teachers and students to become fluent users of inaccurate language and that it leads thereby to a decline in standards. This is not the place for a detailed discussion of this position, simply to note that while all mistakes hamper communication, some hamper it more than others; and that what really hampers communication may not be what we traditionally call 'mistakes' at all. This means that if it is the aim of a foreign language teaching programme to produce users of the language who can actually communicate, there may at times be other quite legitimate priorities than the correction and elimination of all mistakes. Nothing is more destructive of communication than inarticulate even if totally accurate production. 'Having a go' at least gives the listener something to work on from which communication may emerge; tongue-tied reticence kills communication irretrievably.

This over-strong presentation of the communicative case implies it may indeed be less rigorous than alternative approaches in terms of the standards it expects from learners; it also implies that a mistake is something tangible and discrete, something that the teacher can identify and treat or ignore as seems appropriate. In the second part of the chapter I would like to counter both these implications.

COMMUNICATIVE TASKS AND DEGREES OF SKILL

One of the most striking characteristics of the communicative approach to foreign language teaching is that it is essentially task-based. Learning to use the language involves learning to do things through the language; students learn to do things by practising the purposeful use of language in the performance of tasks of various kinds.

Tasks may focus on the practice of specific aspects of the language (e.g. information-gap activities practising asking for information), or they may be much more open-ended (e.g. a simulation involving the production of a radio programme). What they have in common is the production of language for some defined purpose within a defined context. It is the introduction of these two elements, purpose and context, which actually sets communicative teaching apart from non-communicative approaches, and makes the requirements imposed upon the communicative learner ultimately much more stringent than those placed upon the more traditional learner. Whereas the requirements of a grammatical approach can be satisfied simply by the production of grammatically accurate sentences, a communicative approach requires learners to be able to handle in addition appropriacy. On one level, this is a relatively straightforward matter of using the right level of language for the context, e.g. knowing when to use *tu* and when to use *vous*. But on another level it is a much more complex matter of being able to use appropriate language strategies to get what you want, or to make it clear exactly what you mean. How do you express justifiable anger in such a way that it will be recognised as such? How do you complain, advise or enquire so that the addressee knows that is what you are doing? For many school-aged learners of a foreign language, these are difficult enough problems in their own language. To tackle them in a foreign language requires skills that far transcend the relatively simple ability to handle grammar in a non-contextualised way.

A communicative approach is then certainly not a soft option. But how do we set about evaluating student performance on tasks? How do we assess appropriacy? And if mere grammar is not enough, surely it has a role to play – but along with what else?

In a series of task-based EFL examinations developed by the University of Cambridge Local Examinations Syndicate (Certificates of Communicative Skills in English), we have started from the premise that a task may be tackled at a number of different levels by learners at different stages in their learning. The difference between an elementary learner and an advanced one is not the tasks they are able to attempt, but the degree of skill with which they are able to perform them. This seems to reflect real life to the extent that both the 12-year-old on a first trip to France and the French teacher accompanying the trip may wish to go into a shop to buy a souvenir. But presumably the teacher will be able to do it 'better'. What does 'better' mean? Is it just a question of making fewer mistakes?

The criteria for performance at each level are defined. The factors are:

Accuracy
Appropriacy
Range

Flexibility
Size

These factors include some which focus on product (accuracy, appropriacy, size) and some which focus on process (flexibility, range). But only the first two in the list are ones which we can associate with the notion of 'mistake'. It is difficult to get out the red pen and circle mistakes in range, flexibility or size. They do not exist in isolation and cannot be added up in the way beloved of examiners (and teachers) from time immemorial. And yet these three are arguably just as significant as are more conventional measures in forming judgements about the intelligibility of a piece of language produced by a student, whether in an examination or in a real-life interaction with a native speaker. If we set ourselves standards which include these other factors, which are largely left out of account in approaches which emphasise surface accuracy above all else, we can perhaps afford to be more realistic about the more conventional measures of acceptability. In this case the role of the 'mistake' as it is commonly understood can be put in its place as just one (arguably minor) element in the total make-up of a student's use of the foreign language. In other words, if a learner is to communicate effectively, it is just as important (at least) to be able to take the initiative in a conversation using an appropriate range of language, as it is to avoid all mistakes. At advanced levels of language proficiency, of course one can do both; what concerns most of us is how objectives within the reach of 'ordinary' learners can be phrased.

Our specification of realistic objectives for 'effective' oral communication shows that this involves much, much more than the absence of 'mistakes', and that in most cases 'mistakes' are an accepted and expected element of genuine interaction.

It is essential, if the communicative movement is to develop further, that we are able to gain acceptance for this position and are able to show that qualitative descriptions of language performance of this sort are much more useful than quantitative listings of mistakes made. Furthermore we need to gain acceptance for the view that the expectations of student language performance implicit in such descriptions are much more realistic and valid than ones based on idealised grammatical competence.

There may be some way to go yet – but we're on the way.

NOTES

1 Corder, S.P. (1981) *Error Analysis and Interlanguage*, Oxford University Press.
2 For a very interesting discussion of this area, see 'Mistake correction' by Keith Johnson in *English Language Teaching Journal*, 42/2 April 1988.

Part III

The language learner in the classroom

Chapter 8

Differentiation in the foreign language classroom

Bernadette Holmes

WHAT IS DIFFERENTIATION REALLY ABOUT?

Taking the literal definition, differentiation is the process by which we recognise and respond to differences. In the context of the classroom this means:

(a) Getting to know and understand our pupils as learners;
(b) Identifying their individual needs; and then,
(c) Reviewing our teaching styles and materials;
(d) Designing a programme of learning to match those needs. Successful differentiation is about achieving the closest match.

How do our pupils differ?

Every pupil comes to the classroom with differences in experience and attitudes, ability and interests. We need these differences to work for us not against us.

Differences in experience and attitudes

All pupils will have different experience of the world outside the classroom. Existing knowledge of the world often remains an under-exploited resource in the foreign language classroom. The more we can personalise our classroom activities and draw on the wealth of experience unique to each individual, the more relevant learning becomes. In this way we enable pupils to build conceptual bridges between what goes on in the foreign language and real life.

Previous classroom experience can significantly colour attitudes. This is just as much the case for pupils at point of transfer from the primary school as it is for more established pupils of the foreign language. Some pupils will have a very positive self-image. They will regard themselves as successful learners and will actively seek to build on existing achievements. Others may have already experienced failure. It is essential, therefore, that the activities we offer are on the one hand sufficiently challenging to be perceived as worthwhile and on the other hand readily achievable.

All pupils will have previous experience of different teaching and learning styles. The majority of pupils emerge from the primary classroom with the ability to

> work independently;
> work with a partner;
> work with a group;
> organise time;
> manage resources;
> plan activities with other pupils and their teacher; and evaluate their own achievement.

These social and study skills are fundamental to the successful foreign language learner and are recognised in the national curriculum Programmes of Study. A differentiated approach will employ all of these skills separately and in combination at various times. For these pupils, the new element that we are introducing is the ability to communicate in the foreign language. We should not, in theory at least, be introducing new ways of managing the learning, but should be building on existing processes fostered by the primary experience.

As for more established learners of the foreign language, it cannot be taken for granted that they will be accustomed to more flexible ways of learning. Often disappointing responses from pupils to differentiated approaches can be explained by under-developed personal, social and study skills rather than by any linguistic difficulties in the activities themselves. Such pupils will require support in developing increased responsibility in managing their own learning, as well as support in foreign language acquisition.

Some primary pupils may already have experience of learning French as part of their broader curriculum. More generally, pupils at any stage of their learning may have regular contact with France or French speakers outside of the classroom. If this is the case we need to capitalise on this in the design and organisation of pair and group activities. It is helpful to look on existing experience of the foreign language, country and culture not as an inconvenience but as a valuable additional resource.

Differences in levels of attainment and interests

Approximately 2 per cent of the school population will have to live with difficulties in learning at all times. These pupils are subject to Statements under the Education Act 1981. Not all of the 2 per cent will be in Special Education; there may well be statemented pupils in the foreign language classroom. The study of a foreign language is an entitlement in the national curriculum for all pupils and rightly so. Learning a foreign language is one of those rare and welcome opportunities which affords pupils with learning difficulties a fresh start. For a short time, at the outset at least, they are on equal terms with their peers.

Unfortunately, where differentiated approaches are not in place, the needs of statemented pupils often remain unmet. The presence of a statemented pupil should be viewed as a bonus to planning for differentiation. The proper study of individual needs and the development of appropriate teaching strategies should be the foundation stone upon which all classroom practice is based. By analysing foreign language activities and breaking them down into small achievable steps, we begin to perceive what constitutes difficulty and conversely what constitutes achievement. Linguistic progress is a continuum, acknowledging the learning gains of all learners.

Nearly all pupils will experience some difficulty in learning a foreign language at some stage during their five years of study. The difficulties will vary. Some will be short term, for example:

- a temporary hearing loss which affects performance in whole class listening, pair and group activities;
- a period of absence which affects content coverage;
- emotional disturbances in school or at home, resulting in loss of self-esteem, lapses in concentration, reluctance to participate in role play or language games, failure to complete homework, etc.

Some will be longer term but only affect a particular skill; for example, low levels of literacy in the mother tongue may affect the development of literacy in the foreign language and require specific techniques to overcome them; speech difficulties which respond to therapy may affect communication skills and require sensitive handling in the classroom.

What is very clear is that pupils have different learning styles:

- some pupils respond to visual stimulus while others have limited visual memory;
- some have strong auditory memory and recall language almost by virtue of its musical properties, while others do not;
- many pupils tend to make swift progress if they are actively involved in the presentation of new language, for example, whole class mime, rhythmic chanting, active demonstration of meaning. For some pupils such approaches are less appropriate. Boys in general tend to react less favourably than girls to written tasks. They prefer active, practical learning related to clear contexts, purposes and results. Girls appear less willing to take risks and often miss opportunities to take the initiative in whole class activities.

To cater for differences in learning styles and to combat stereotyping, the differentiated classroom should provide variety and balance in the different types of experience offered. There needs to be a range of collaborative activities in which boys and girls can work together. Roles and responsibilities in group work need to be clearly defined and involve boys and girls in investigative activities, problem-solving opportunities, tasks involving information technology. Opportunities which enable pupils of different abilities to work together constructively should be sought.

What is undeniable is the motivational impact of classroom activities which are based upon pupils' personal interests. Irrespective of differences in ability, achievement is significantly enhanced by harnessing the enthusiasm which pupils invest in their own intrinsic interests. If we take this into account as we design particular activities, we can allow as many outlets for creative energy as there are pupils in the class. In this way one well-designed activity could allow scope for thirty individualised learning experiences.

How do you plan for differentiation? Is it feasible?

In some ways it is quite a straightforward matter to accept that pupils differ in terms of their experience, attitudes, levels of ability and range of interests, but as a new teacher faced with a class of thirty pupils, it can seem a daunting prospect to accept responsibility for meeting the different learning needs of each individual, and then multiply that by the number of other pupils in other classes! Where do you start?

Once we recognise certain fundamental principles underpinning differentiation, for example that:

all pupils are different;
all pupils are capable of learning;
not all pupils learn in the same way;
all pupils have different rates of progress;

it almost seems unreasonable to have ever expected all pupils to learn by the same means.

Our first response as we plan for differentiation must be a willingness to modify our own practice. Much can be achieved by variety in

the ways we present new language;
the ways we practise new language and make it relevant to the pupils' direct first-hand experience;
the range of contexts, activities and experiences which we offer to consolidate and apply the learning.

(see Holmes 1991)

Flexibility is the key to differentiation. To accommodate flexible approaches to managing the learning, we may have to make a cultural shift in our own attitudes. We need to feel comfortable with the characteristics of a differentiated classroom:

> there will be a choice of activities;
> not all pupils will be engaged upon the same activity at the same time;
> pupils will not always work with the same partner or in the same group;
> pupils will move more freely around the classroom;
> pupils will have more open access to equipment and reference materials;
> pupils will make a contribution to assessing their own work.

How do you differentiate classroom activity?

Rules of thumb

The kinds of activities that we offer in the classroom can be differentiated in a number of ways. We have to ask ourselves certain general questions about what constitutes difficulty. For instance:

(a) In spoken tasks are pupils required to
- initiate communication?
- assume a false identity?
- use formal rather than familiar language?
- adopt a different mood or state of mind?
- solve a problem?
- discuss choices?

(b) In both listening and reading tasks, we should consider challenges presented by the choice of text itself, for example:

In listening tasks we should listen for
- the speed and length of text;
- the number of speakers involved;
- non-standard pronunciation;
- background noise.

In both listening and reading tasks, we should ask
- to what extent is the content of the text familiar and relevant to the experience of the pupils?
- to what degree would sociocultural differences influence understanding?
- is key information repeated in a number of ways to assist understanding?
- do pupils need to reorganise or classify information?
- how much redundant language do pupils have to sift through in order to discover key information?
- to what extent does the successful completion of the task rely on memory?

(c) In writing tasks, we should look at
  - the amount of language pupils are expected to produce,
    e.g. single items to fill in gaps, forms or labels
      short phrases to convey a message
      short cohesive passages as in a description, postcard, diary entry, brochure, etc.
  - are the activities independent or do they involve adapting language from model examples?
(d) In all cases we should consider the nature of support provided:
  - do pupils have access to appropriate reference materials, e.g. self-help sheets, exercise books, textbooks, dictionaries, if required?
  - are strategies in place to enable intervention from other pupils or members of staff, if needed?
(e) The layout of any materials we use can affect the degree of difficulty.

(see Holmes 1991)

DIFFERENTIATION BY TASK

Taking all of these criteria into consideration, we will develop a greater sensitivity to what makes activities challenging. We will know how to simplify activities or increase the level of challenge.

When we choose to differentiate by task, we should already have a clear idea of what successful completion of the task will be and what evidence of achievement it will yield. It is helpful if pupils know what they have achieved and can be involved in evaluating their own progress.

These are some examples taken from the foreign language classroom:

Topic: Directions

Attainment target 1   Listening

Task at Level 3
Pupils are given an unmarked street plan and listen to a simple taped message giving instructions of how to get from the station to various places in the town e.g. swimming pool, cinema etc.

Successful completion of the task will be demonstrated by labelling the correct places on the map and comparing with an original copy.

Attainment target 2   Speaking

Pair work task at Level 3
Pupil A has a street plan with five places marked on it and Pupil B has a complementary street plan with a further five places marked on it. By taking

it in turns to ask and answer questions, each partner fills in the missing five places by following their partner's directions.

Successful completion will be demonstrated by the partners comparing their finished maps, which should be identical by the end of the activity.

Attainment target 3   Reading

Task at Level 3
From a defined range of language, pupils read clues for a simple treasure hunt.

They mark on a map where various items of treasure are to be found.

They check their versions against an original copy.

Attainment target 4   Writing

Task at Level 3
Using a simple map and the same defined range of language as in the reading task, pupils create clues for a simple treasure hunt for other pupils to complete.

Their finished versions are assessed by the teacher.

Becoming familiar with the programmes of study and the ability to attribute particular activities to particular statements of attainment is already a significant first step in beginning the process of planning for differentiation. However, when we use differentiated tasks, we have already predetermined the potential level of achievement by the nature of the tasks themselves. This can eventually cause problems for us and for the pupils. We should bear in mind that even if pupils start out at the same place in their learning, by virtue of their own inherent differences and in response to the learning process itself there will rapidly be disparity in their rates of progress. This is equally true of setted classes as it is of mixed attainment classes. There is no such thing as a homogeneous class. If we are intending to differentiate by task, we should cater for this disparity in our lesson planning. It will be helpful to prepare supplementary activities or to seek them out from published materials.

It is suggested in the Non-Statutory Guidance (NCC 1992) that we manage differentiation by planning under three broad objectives:

- core objectives – these refer to what the whole class should be able to do;
- reinforcement objectives – these involve the kinds of activity which offer pupils opportunities to work at earlier levels or practice particular skills in a variety of ways;
- extension objectives – these include activities which accelerate the learning for high-attaining pupils and avoid the frustration of unchallenging work.

Particularly as we design extension objectives, we will be looking at more creative activities which show achievement at different levels.

DIFFERENTIATION BY OUTCOME

In this case, the activity does not restrict or prescribe the quality of outcome. The level of success is decided by matching the response against descriptions of performance.

For example, for homework, pupils are invited to make a short tape expressing their feelings about school life.

Pupil A is able to list a range of subjects and express some simple opinions. Pupil B is able to list a range of subjects, express and justify opinions, and uses a wider range of vocabulary and structure.

By referring to the statements of attainment for Attainment target 2 Speaking, Pupil A will have shown the ability to operate at Level 3. Pupil B will have shown the ability to operate at Level 4.

The activity, then, can be thought of as open-ended, allowing pupils to achieve at their own level.

Implementing core, reinforcement and extension activities in the classroom

Returning to the topic of Directions and the four example activities which differentiate by task, we could think of these as the core objectives. We know that some pupils in the class will achieve these very quickly and others will struggle. So our responsibility as organiser of the learning is twofold:

(i)   to find ways to modify the activities and make them accessible for low-attaining pupils;
(ii) to provide other activities which stretch high-attaining pupils.

Some examples of reinforcement activities

Pupils who will have difficulties with the listening and speaking tasks could benefit from some warm-up activities which prepare the way step by step to the core objectives.

(a)   They may need to practise the names of places around the town. This could be done by playing snap with some symbol picture cards; to win the pair you must identify the place in French first.
(b)   The same symbol cards could then be used in combination with a simple grid map. In pairs, Partner A decides where particular places are and puts their symbols on the grid. Partner B is not allowed to look at the original plan, but listens to Partner A giving the directions, places the symbols onto the grid and then compares. As the symbols are movable,

they can be set and reset. Pupils can use the activity to practise language as many times as they wish. No reading or writing is involved.

(c) The written word for places around the town can be introduced on a set of differently coloured cards. In a small group a game of pairs can be played with all the cards face up. Pupils take it in turns to match up the appropriate word with the matching symbol picture. The second version is to play a memory game where all the cards are face down. Pupils turn up a pair of cards and if they match they have won the pair; if they do not match they turn them over again. To win they will need to recall where the appropriate pairs of cards are placed. The same games can be played with symbol cards and labels for simple directions.

(d) The written task can be assisted by supplying self-help material, for example, a sheet with symbol pictures and a defined range of language to be used to create the treasure hunt. The treasure hunt can be based on the same simple grid map used in the speaking task.

An example of an extension activity

Pupils could create a treasure hunt of their own design. They can be encouraged to use more descriptive language, seeking help from reference materials, including a bilingual dictionary, or working with the support of the foreign language assistant. As they create their treasure hunt, they will be experimenting with new language and stepping beyond the defined range of expression used in the core task. The beauty of this is that pupils acquire new language in a context that they control and create.

The activity can be personalised by using simple maps or photos of a town or area of their choice. This can be in England or a place in France that the pupils know, or anywhere else that means something to them. A good example used photographs of the beach in Jamaica! One group devised a cunning plan; the treasure comprised a series of page and reference numbers in a French mail order catalogue. The treasure hunters had to use reference skills to discover what the items of treasure were – luxury goods, compact discs, silk lingerie, etc.

At a later stage, these activities can become learning materials for other pupils in the class. The individual designers remain with a group of treasure hunters and help them to understand new vocabulary and find the loot! They would carry this out using the target language as much as possible. This can offer an ideal way of rearranging working groups so that low-attaining pupils work with higher-attaining pupils. The benefit to the high attainers is that they apply the new language they have acquired through reading and writing to a fresh context where all four language skills are in action. The benefit to the low attainers is often an increase in motivation, which is just as important as linguistic gains. They want to understand the language and solve the treasure hunt simply because they do not want to lose face with their peers.

Resource implications

Clearly the more resources we have the more we can do. With a computer and concept keyboard overlay, clues for the treasure hunt can be at different levels of difficulty to accelerate progress in reading. With sufficient tape-recorders and microphone facilities, pupils can record their own clues onto tape and other pupils can solve the clues by listening, using a junction box and headsets. The foreign language assistant, if available, can record different versions of a treasure hunt at three levels of complexity.

Conclusions

From the drawing board to the classroom

Once we have a clear idea of the learning objectives, have taken stock of our resources and prepared a range of learning materials, it only remains for us to set up the activities and support individual pupils or groups through a sequence of learning. The more experience we have of a differentiated approach, the better we become at managing the classroom. To implement the given examples of core, reinforcement and extension activities, we have to make certain decisions about which pupils do what and when. We have to make choices about how we organise the learning sequence. For example:

(a) The linear sequence
All pupils in the class work lockstep towards the core objectives.
Lesson 1
    Presentation of new language
    Listening task
    Pair work task
    Reading task
    Writing task
Lesson 2
    Following an evaluation of different pupils' achievements, pupils work in groups on appropriate reinforcement or extension activities, according to their level of attainment.
    The disadvantages to this approach are that some pupils will fail almost from the presentation onwards. Others will be restricted by, for example, having to listen to the taped material several times for the benefit of low-attaining pupils. There will none the less be clear objectives and differentiation of experience in terms of the four attainment targets by the end of the two lessons.

(b) 50 per cent linear sequence/50 per cent group work
Lesson 1
    Whole class presentation
    Whole class listening

50 per cent of the pupils begin the reading and writing tasks
50 per cent of the pupils begin the pair work task, allowing the teacher to support individual pupils and assess their levels of attainment.
As pupils complete the pair work they move onto the reading and writing tasks and vice versa.

Lesson 2

Appropriate reinforcement or extension tasks are introduced. There are already certain advantages in this model, as the teacher is more able to diagnose the capabilities of individuals and offer support as immediate needs arise. However, differentiation is still retrospective and is not fully in place until the second lesson.

(c) The carousel model

Lesson 1

Active presentation with some involvement of higher-attaining pupils in demonstrating subsequent tasks to the whole class. Multi-activity work in groups, for example:

1   Six pupils listening on headsets; pupils control the tape and wind it back as many times as required.
2   Six pupils working in pairs.
3   Six pupils working on the reading task.
4   Six more able pupils directed to the writing task first.
5   Six pupils with learning difficulties working on the reinforcement activities, assisted for some of the time by the teacher or another adult, e.g. support teacher or foreign language assistant.

On completion of one activity, the group as a whole moves on to the next activity.

Lesson 2

The carousel continues with further opportunities to complete reinforcement and core activities, as appropriate, and with the gradual introduction of extension activities.

This model is often the favoured starting place for more flexible approaches. Pupils are working more independently of the teacher and can assess their own work. The disadvantages are that:

– the pace is often controlled by the average rate of progress of the group as a whole;
– pupils with learning difficulties are noticeably excluded from the main hub of activity;
– higher-attaining pupils are obliged to work through the core activities, which in some cases may not be necessary.

(d) Differentiation by guided choice

Active presentation as in the carousel model.
Multi-activity group work.
In this case, pupils choose from a menu of all the prepared materials activities best suited to their needs.

- Lower-attaining pupils might choose from the range of games;
- Pupils might move at their own pace through the core objectives, organising the equipment and materials themselves and assessing their work on completion of the activities. If they need further practice, they can choose from the range of reinforcement games, before attempting the core activity again;
- Higher-attaining pupils might be directed to extension activities immediately, if appropriate, and thereby subsume the core objectives.

This model of differentiation is the most advanced and places the greatest demands on the pupils in terms of maturity and responsibility. Teachers who adopt this model gradually build up banks of differentiated materials and activities. They often favour a 'pick and mix' approach to published materials rather than follow one textbook only. Pupils in partnership with their teachers begin to plan an appropriate route through the learning.

Once in place, this model can prove to be the most successful:

- the pace is manageable and varied according to individual needs;
- there are resource implications, but pupils are involved in generating their own learning materials to some extent;
- activities are engrossing in themselves;
- pupils are stimulated and achieving at a range of different levels.

In all the models it can be seen that we are not confining our preparations to a given lesson but to a series of lessons. We are making decisions about the kind of stimulus we use, the equipment we require, the eventual destination of all our pupils.

Organising for differentiation can sometimes feel a little bit like organising the London Marathon. There are all sorts of competitors of different levels on the same course. Some will need the physiotherapist or the Red Cross tent more than once along the route, others will complete the course far faster than the rest and will already be preparing for the next, more challenging fixture. But there are some interesting features about the London Marathon that make all the effort worthwhile:

- every competitor's performance is valued;
- often competitors support each other over the finishing line;
- competitors can complete the course in their own time;
- each achieves a personal best.

That is what differentiation is all about, isn't it?

REFERENCES

Holmes, B. (1991) *Communication Re-activated*, London: CILT.
National Curriculum Council (1992) *Modern Foreign Languages Non-Statutory Guidance*, National Curriculum Council.

Chapter 9

Autonomy in language learning
Some theoretical and practical considerations

David Little

WHAT IS LEARNER AUTONOMY?

Five negatives

- Autonomy is *not* a synonym for self-instruction; in other words, autonomy is *not* limited to learning without a teacher.
- In the classroom context, autonomy does *not* entail an abdication of responsibility on the part of the teacher; it is *not* a matter of letting the learners get on with things as best they can.
- On the other hand, autonomy is *not* something that teachers do to learners; that is, it is *not* another teaching method.
- Autonomy is *not* a single, easily described behaviour.
- Autonomy is *not* a steady state achieved by learners.

A provisional definition

Learner autonomy is essentially a matter of the learner's psychological relation to the process and content of learning. We recognise it in a wide variety of behaviours as a capacity for detachment, critical reflection, decision-making and independent action. The various freedoms that autonomy implies are always conditional and constrained, never absolute. As social beings our independence is always balanced by dependence, our essential condition is one of interdependence; total detachment is a principal determining feature not of autonomy but of autism.

APPROACHES TO AUTONOMY IN LANGUAGE LEARNING

General educational arguments for autonomy

If democratic states are to develop and flourish as democracies, they must undertake educational measures calculated to develop the capacity of their citizens to think and act as free and self-determining individuals (see Holec

1981). We cannot expect children and adolescents to mature into autonomous adults if we do not give them the opportunity to behave autonomously as they learn.

Psychological arguments for autonomy

Each of us learns by assimilating new information in terms of what he or she already knows (cp. Barnes 1976, Britton 1972, Kelly 1963; also Schank & Abelson 1977, Anderson & Pearson 1984). Arguably, then, the most efficient learners will be those who know how to bring their existing knowledge to bear on each new learning task – in other words, who have developed a degree of psychological autonomy.

Classroom learning involves two kinds of interaction: the internal psychological interaction between new and existing knowledge, and the external social interaction by which new knowledge is mediated and learners can negotiate their way towards new meanings. Pedagogical measures calculated to promote learner autonomy within the social dimension will certainly support, but they may also in turn actually promote, the development of autonomy within the psychological dimension.

Autonomy and successful language use

If language learners are to be efficient communicators in their target language, they must be autonomous to the extent of having sufficient independence, self-reliance and self-confidence to fulfil the variety of social, psychological and discourse roles in which they will be cast. This entails being aware of the socio-pragmatic requirements of the different situations in which they are called upon to use the target language; sensitive to the varying psychological relations they will have to the different persons with whom they must communicate; and capable equally of taking initiatives in communication and responding to the initiatives of others.

Genuinely communicative approaches recognise that it is not enough to *teach* by *telling* and *showing*; we must create the conditions in which our learners can *learn* by *doing*, that is, by *communicating*. It is thus a fundamental requirement of the communicative classroom that it should be capable of accommodating a wide variety of discourse types in order that learners have the opportunity of filling the widest possible variety of discourse roles *as they learn*. Of course, this kind of flexibility follows naturally from the practice of genuine learner-centredness.

Autonomy, language acquisition and language processing

Research into first language acquisition has highlighted the importance of interaction between the child and its parents, siblings, care givers, and so on.

But it has also shown that the units of a language are acquired in a predictable order and that the child moves from one stage of acquisition to the next only when it is ready to do so. In the sense that its progress is only partly determined by environmental stimuli of one kind or another, the child acquiring its first language enjoys a degree of autonomy. This is not to say that the child exercises conscious control over the acquisition process; but it is to say that vital transitions in first language development occur when the child is ready, and not when its parents (for example) say they should.

These facts have two lessons for second and foreign language teachers:

- They should remind us that there is a crucial sense in which all learning is internal to the learner. However much we consult with our learners about learning targets and how best to achieve them, and however flexible we are in the way we arrange the furniture and organise the discourse of our classrooms, we cannot control what goes on inside each learner's head. What is more, learners require time and psychological space in which to learn; and if we are too insistently interventionist in our pedagogical practice we can all too easily deprive them of that time and space.
- Like children learning their first language, learners of second and foreign languages follow predictable routes of acquisition. Research evidence seems to suggest that pedagogical intervention can provide an important underpinning for natural acquisition processes (for an accessible account of relevant research findings, see Littlewood 1984); but as with all learning, so with language acquisition, the teacher's influence stops a long way short of being absolute. Thus again, the most successful learners will be those who have developed sufficient autonomy (in my original psychological definition) to allow those processes free rein.

The development of literacy skills entails the development of the capacity to plan, monitor and edit discourse – the capacity to produce texts of various kinds via internal and only partly recoverable processes of interaction with oneself. Planning, monitoring and editing depend on detachment – in this case from language itself and from the emerging linguistic product. They are thus another aspect of the successful language user's autonomy. For language users who are also language learners, the reflective processes that planning, monitoring and editing embody are a means of providing crucial conscious support for the essentially unconscious processes of acquisition.

AUTONOMY IN TWO CONTRASTING LEARNING CONTEXTS

Autonomy can manifest itself in a great variety of ways. This is because the freedoms it entails are always conditional and constrained by the various factors that determine the context in which it arises. Accordingly, if we want to promote learner autonomy in our particular environment, we need to be aware of the conditions and constraints that will define the limits of what can be achieved.

Autonomous learning outside the full-time educational system

Adults learning outside the full-time educational system in order to fulfil some precise personal or professional need will set their own learning targets and decide when sufficient learning has taken place. Because their needs are precise, they may well not be met by conventional learning materials, in which case they will have to collect materials of their own – in all probability authentic materials. They will then have to decide how to go about learning from such materials, and it will be up to them to organise their learning so that it fits in with all their other commitments.

Such learners clearly enjoy at least the possibility of autonomy in every aspect of their learning. But like all learners, they are by definition inexpert in relation to their learning targets, so that they are likely to need guidance of various kinds. For this reason, most schemes designed to promote autonomous language learning among adults are founded on a combination of learning resources and learner counselling (for a discussion of some of the fundamental issues, see Riley 1985 and Little 1989; for a case study, see Little & Grant 1986). Learner counselling aims to help learners achieve an ever-clearer understanding of why they are learning, what they are learning, and how they are learning.

Autonomous learning within the educational system

For those inside the system it can easily appear that there are so many constraints, so many factors over which learners (and teachers) have no control, that learner autonomy is impossible. But to take such a view is to fall into the trap of confusing autonomy with self-instruction, to identify its freedoms exclusively with external matters of organisation, and to forget that autonomy is essentially a matter of the psychological relation between the learner and the content and process of learning.

Teachers enjoy – and will continue to enjoy – a large measure of freedom, first in interpreting the aims of the syllabus, then in deciding how best to fulfil them in terms of content and method. The question is, are they prepared to share this freedom with their pupils?

PRACTICAL ISSUES IN THE IMPLEMENTATION OF AUTONOMY

The teacher

It is not easy for teachers to change their role from purveyor of information to counsellor and manager of learning resources. It is not easy for teachers to stop talking: after all, if they stop talking they stop teaching, and if they stop teaching, their learners may stop learning. And it is not easy for teachers to let learners solve problems for themselves; for that takes time, and there is always so much ground to cover. Committing oneself to learner autonomy requires a lot of nerve.

The learner

Autonomy – accepting responsibility for their own learning – may be the last thing learners want. In many cases their chief interest is in acquitting themselves well in the exams, and it may be difficult to shake their belief that the teacher's job is straightforwardly to prepare them for that end. This can be a problem especially with more able pupils, who tend to feel comfortable in a state of more or less total dependence provided their efforts are duly rewarded.

We should not be surprised if some learners are resistant to autonomy; for autonomy implies a continuous challenge to our certainties, and that can be very unsettling. But always it will be the autonomous learners who most easily make the transition from learner to learner/user of the target language.

Determining the content of learning

Conventional language coursebooks can certainly be used in the autonomous classroom, but they are too constraining to serve as the sole focus of learning. For one thing, autonomous learners must be able to range freely in their choice of learning materials and learning tasks; for another, classroom discourse arising from language teaching materials has a strong tendency to focus on issues of grammar and interactional structure, so that whatever meaning gets communicated is always filtered through a concern for form (see Devitt 1989). By contrast, non-pedagogical language use always gives meaning priority over form.

The individual and group project work that forms a central part of learning activity in any autonomous classroom finds its most satisfactory focus in authentic materials, e.g. the *Authentik* newspapers and cassettes, all kinds of printed material, radio, satellite television. But learning activities in the autonomous classroom also need to be supported by some kind of resource centre that embraces the spoken as well as the written language and ideally is equipped with audio, video and computer technologies (for discussion on how to establish and run such a centre, see Little 1989).

Learning how to learn

It is essential to the development of autonomy that learners become aware of themselves as learners – aware, for example, of the learning techniques they instinctively favour and capable of judging how effective those techniques are. Successful autonomous learning schemes in Scandinavia have found a solution in the learner's journal, in which each learner keeps an individual record of the learning undertaken and assesses how well or badly particular tasks have been done.

But journals are not enough in themselves. Learners will need to be helped to a greater understanding of the learning processes in which they are involved. The supplement to the September 1989 issue of the *Authentik* newspapers provides various kinds of information not usually put in the way of learners; while Gail Ellis and Barbara Sinclair's *Learning to learn English* (1989) contains a wealth of practical ideas that can easily be adapted for learners of other languages.

CONCLUSION

Learner autonomy is not easy to achieve, and for that reason alone it poses a very great challenge to teachers. Yet it is a challenge we must respond to positively. In general, autonomous learners are defined by the fact that they can integrate what they learn with the rest of what they are. In the special case of second and foreign languages, this process of integration means that autonomous learners are in the fullest sense users of the language they are learning. It is through autonomy that our learners will fulfil the communicative aims of their second or foreign language curricula. Perhaps more important in the broader educational perspective, it is through autonomy that they will learn to be 'the artists of their own lives' (Ignatieff 1990).

REFERENCES

Anderson, R.C. and P.D. Pearson: 'A schematheoretic view of basic processes in reading comprehension'. In P.D. Pearson (ed.), *Handbook of reading research*, pp. 255–91, Longman. (1984)

Barnes D.: *From communication to curriculum*, Penguin. (1976)

Britton, J.: *Language and learning*, Penguin. (1972) (First published 1970 by Allen Lane, The Penguin Press.)

Devitt, S.M.: 'Classroom discourse: its nature and its potential for language learning', *CLCS Occasional Paper No. 21*, Trinity College, Dublin, Centre for Language and Communication Studies. (1989)

Ellis, G. and B. Sinclair: *Learning to learn English: a course in learner training*, Cambridge University Press. (1989)

Holec, H.: *Autonomy and foreign language learning*, Pergamon. (1981) (First published 1979 by Council of Europe, Strasbourg.)

Ignatieff, M.: 'We are the artists of our own lives', *The Observer*, 7 January 1990.

Kelly, G.: *A theory of personality*, Norton. (1963)

Little, D.G. (ed.): *Self-access systems for language learning*, Authentik, Dublin, in association with CILT, London. (1989)

Little, D., S.M. Devitt and D. Singleton: *Learning foreign languages from Authentic texts: theory and practice*, Authentik, Dublin, in association with CILT, London. (1989)

Little, D.G. and A.J. Grant: 'Learning German without a teacher. Report on a self-instructional programme for undergraduate students of Engineering Science at Trinity College, Dublin, 1982–1984'. *CLCS Occasional Paper No. 14*, Trinity College, Dublin, Centre for Language and Communication Studies. (1986)

Littlewood, W.T.: *Foreign and second language learning*, Cambridge University Press. (1984)

Riley, P. (ed.): *Discourse and learning*, Longman. (1985)

Schank, R.C. and R.P. Abelson: 'Scripts, plans and knowledge.' In P. Johnson-Laird and P.C. Wason (eds): *Thinking. Readings in cognitive science*, Cambridge University Press. (1977)

Sinclair, J.McH. and M. Coulthard: *Towards an analysis of discourse*, Oxford University Press. (1975)

Trim, J.L.M.: Preface to H. Holec (ed.): *Autonomy and self-directed learning: present fields of application*, Council of Europe, Strasbourg. (1988)

Chapter 10

Extending opportunities

Modern foreign languages for pupils with special educational needs

Barbara Lee

INTRODUCTION

As Montgomery (1990) argues, 'It is not necessarily the curriculum but the pedagogy which is the barrier to the participation of children with learning difficulties.' It is of importance therefore to examine some of the methods and materials in use in both mainstream and special schools. The teaching and learning strategies employed by teachers will depend on factors such as class size, the learning needs of the pupils in the class, the aims of the curriculum, the resources available and the amount of support provided. To a certain extent the personality and style of the teacher will also determine the way in which the class is run.

Many of the questions raised by teachers, considering the most appropriate approaches to teaching pupils with special needs, relate to planning and preparing work schemes which take account of the differing needs of pupils. Approaches which attempt to provide individualised materials and tasks for pupils may seem ideal but the practical realities of large mixed-attainment classes, small classrooms, limited resources and scarce teacher time tend to make such approaches seem unrealistic. The discussion below describes some of the difficulties teachers face and focuses on the strategies and materials being developed which attempt to reconcile the needs of individuals with the demands imposed by the class.

TEACHING AND LEARNING STRATEGIES – MAINSTREAM SCHOOLS

In most mainstream schools pupils are taught in groups of between twenty and thirty pupils, except for specially designated classes for lower-attaining pupils or those with special needs. Pupils are usually taught in similar attainment groups for languages throughout most of key stages 3 and 4; they may start off in mixed-attainment groups but are usually put into broad or narrow sets after a few terms (see, for example, APU (assessment of performance unit) data on class size and organisation, DES/WO, 1985, 1986, 1987).

Much modern language teaching follows a similar pattern of activities, often characterised as presentation, practice and consolidation. An example of how this might be enacted in a typical classroom is shown below:

1 The teacher conducts an oral session with the whole class, sometimes to introduce new material, sometimes to revise past or ongoing material;
2 pupils continue to practise the material in pairs or groups, often orally only, sometimes using written materials too;
3 pupils work individually, in pairs or groups on tasks which may require listening, reading and/or writing.

Although this is clearly a simplified version of a lesson, it does, nevertheless, identify the main types of activity and the areas where consideration can be given to ways of ensuring that what goes on is accessible to all the pupils in a class.

Teacher talk

Many language teachers are used to classes which contain pupils of supposedly similar attainment, and may therefore feel that they can teach the whole class from the front without difficulty. However, any group contains pupils who have a range of strengths and weaknesses, and the phenomenon described by Montgomery (1990) is common in setted classes too, 'It is common practice to teach to the middle of a mixed-ability group. It is assumed that by means of this strategy two-thirds of the children are reached. Most teachers then give 'the less able' extra attention to help them over any difficulties (Hegarty *et al.* 1981). The able pupils in this scheme receive little or no attention at all.'

This lack of attentiveness by the teacher to the needs of all the pupils in the class was apparent in a lesson observed by the present researcher, described below:

The first part of the lesson consisted of an oral question and answer session, conducted by the teacher in a mixture of French and English. To an observer, sitting at the back of the room, it was plain that some pupils were fully involved in the activity, listening to the questions and thinking about the answers, others were listening some of the time, usually when they heard words they recognised, and a few were barely paying attention and only joined in when the teacher got the whole class to repeat in chorus a question or an answer.

Throughout the course of the oral sections of this lesson (which lasted 1 hour 10 minutes) the same pattern could be observed, except that as the lesson went on so the pupils who were not following made less and less attempt to sit quietly but began to talk to each other and pupils sitting nearby. During the reading and writing activities, when help was provided to the pupils with learning difficulties, they were able to fulfil the task by picking out the relevant words and phrases and by completing the grid.

Clearly these pupils were able to participate in the learning activities when individual support was provided but were unable to play an active part in the class activities when special attention was not provided.

In another class observed, the same difficulties were apparent:

The class was known as a lower-attaining, difficult group, the time of day and length of lesson were not favourable, and the teacher was clearly not at ease with the class. Towards the end of the lesson, the pupils were working in pairs and individually to match German words with pictures; some were concentrating, some had finished and were chatting and amusing themselves noisily, and others had barely started as they either did not understand what to do or could not do it without help, and they too were joining in with the chatting and playing around.

The teacher, who was attempting to help individuals, tried to move on to the next phase of the learning, and to prepare the background for the homework she was setting. From the front, she tried to get pupils to look at the overhead projector and participate in some question and answer work building on what the pupils had been doing earlier.

Many of the pupils were not listening to what she was saying and certainly not trying to answer the questions; they did not listen when she explained the homework. No doubt many of the class would not do the homework at all or do it badly because they did not know what they were supposed to be doing, or because they could not do it.

Interestingly, the four pupils in the class with statements of educational needs, spent much of their time working separately with the special needs support teacher. Their particular needs appeared to be being catered for whereas many of the other pupils appeared to be learning little. The teacher, too, was aware that the lesson had gone badly and felt that it was unsatisfactory for both her and the pupils.

So how can teachers modify their approach to ensure that all pupils are learning something from the oral phase of the lesson, often crucial for understanding and carrying out activities in the rest of the lesson? Hegarty *et al.* (1981), in their project to investigate the education provided for pupils with special needs in ordinary schools, asked teachers whether they had modified their teaching approach because of the presence of pupils with special needs. They found that 72 per cent of those answering the question (a high number did not answer as they did not teach children with special needs) said they had made some modification. The most common approaches were the following:

- give more individual attention, make more time both personal and academic;
- simplify teaching, give instructions slowly and clearly, break content matter down to its components, work more slowly, set shorter objectives.

These correspond closely with the kinds of approaches suggested by teachers interviewed. A special needs teacher described how she and a modern language colleague had discussed some of the ways in which the modern language teachers could ensure that the pupils with learning difficulties in their classes benefited from the teaching. These included things like encouraging all pupils to put up their hands and participate in question and answer sessions, providing tasks which can be done at different levels, and making sure that materials give clear and unambiguous messages. One language teacher interviewed described a pupil who had become school phobic because of his early experiences of French (in a different school). She explained that

> he wanted to know what was expected in the lesson, so I used to see him in break, before the lesson, and I would tell him what I was going to ask him to do. He wouldn't join in so I said he had got to put up his hand at least once during the lesson. Seeing him like that though, requires time and I can't do it a lot.

A difficult pointed out by a head of special needs is that language teachers who are not familiar with pupils with learning difficulties tend to assume a certain level of general skills on the part of pupils, 'for example, they assume that the pupils will have a pen and will be able to read from the blackboard and copy from the blackboard, things like that which some of these pupils cannot do.'

Another area of difficulty for many pupils is following instructions for activities. An advisory teacher on an in-service training course attended by the present researcher discussed some of the problems experienced by children with learning difficulties: the teacher may give a string of instructions on what to do next, the materials needed, the outcomes expected and so on, and many pupils get lost after the first one. A special needs teacher agreed that this could be confusing, and explained that in the withdrawal groups that she and her colleague taught some of the time, 'we tend to say "get your books out" and we wait until they have all done that before we do the next bit, and give them the next instruction, and even then we repeat it three times.' The advisory teacher suggested that an alternative approach would be to get straight into the task without any preliminary remarks; this would prevent the pupils from switching off, something which often happens if they are subjected to a list of instructions.

In question and answer sessions teachers can ask questions at different levels and encourage the lower-attaining pupils to have a go at answering some questions, at least. Many pupils with learning difficulties tend to have short attention spans and therefore find that long oral sessions are too demanding. One way suggested of helping to retain pupils' concentration was to get them to listen to what other pupils said, make a note to remind themselves of what was said, then get them to repeat or recount what was said earlier.

If a support teacher or classroom assistant is available, he or she can also help individual pupils by whispering explanations or repeating things, so that the pupil can follow, as one teacher explained, 'I shadow for a bit and if the pupil is losing contact with the lesson, I jump in. I have a word with them, I whisper in their ear and so on.'

In addition, less teaching from the front and more teaching to individuals or small groups of pupils was considered helpful for pupils with short attention spans and poor concentration.

Pair and group work

One of the ways in which teachers have tried to cater for the differing needs of pupils, particularly in mixed-attainment classes, is through the differentiation of tasks and materials. Pairs or groups of pupils can be set different tasks to consolidate the oral work carried out by the whole class or pupils can be set the same task but with different or lower level outcomes expected.

Differing amounts of support can also be provided, especially if a special needs teacher is present. One support teacher described how she worked in some classes: 'In the first year I sit with groups and hopefully I could notice what they were doing and help them with things. Then I ask them things and help them decide when they should ask for help from the [language] teacher. I also move to them when I can see they're struggling.'

Moving away from whole-class activities towards paired and group work, however, creates problems of its own. Many teachers have large classes, of 30+ pupils who may have a wide range of learning and behavioural difficulties. Children with statements of special needs may get extra support from a special needs teacher or classroom assistant, but the majority of pupils will be competing for the attention of the teacher. As Montgomery (1990) describes, 'In these circumstances the children with learning difficulties and those who misbehave, often because they cannot cope with the work, absorb most of the teacher's time. The rest must get on as best they can. Practice activities and rest from work are often overextended to fill the time until the teacher can return.'

However, in addition to support from teachers, the materials provided to cue or underpin the task can also be varied so that pupils get the degree of help they need. The section on page 95 describes some of the different ways of presenting and adapting materials for pupils with learning difficulties.

An alternative approach to producing different tasks or materials is for other pupils to provide support. In one school a teacher described how they set up groups, 'We try to have mixed-ability groups so that some better ones will help less able pupils. But mostly, they work in friendship groups which are mixed-ability anyway . . . the lower ability kids are very well looked after by the other kids.' A teacher in another school described his surprise and pleasure that pupils did help each other:

> When I have been on courses and heard people talking about getting the better pupils to help the less good ones, I thought that was all airy-fairy stuff. But in fact I've found that it has actually happened, so that those who have done it [German] before do help the ones who haven't.

Another approach which provides enhanced opportunities for pupils to work at appropriate levels is by increasing the control pupils have over the work they are doing. One teacher described their attempts in that direction:

> We are trying to move away from teacher control to pupil control. The pupils have dictionaries and we are trying to get them to use tape-recorders with headphones. With my current fourth year I was worried about whether the kids would behave OK but in fact, when I did try it out, it worked out fine.

Written tasks

Here too, when pupils are working on reading or writing tasks, help can be provided through the support teacher, other pupils or materials which are appropriate to the individual needs of pupils.

The computer has a role to play here, since activities can be designed so that pupils ask for and get the degree of help they need, without this being predetermined. It also acts as a useful tool for pupils with physical disabilities or learning difficulties who find handwriting impossible or laborious. In one school the use of computers was described thus:

> Kids with special needs are very keen to use wordprocessing. They can type things out so that they look beautiful. The kids also like the laptops a lot so that they can print out their work. We do things like penfriend letters, so someone like Jason does his letter on the computer so that it looks a lot better than by hand.

The use of the computer in this way also provides motivation to pupils who might otherwise be reluctant to practise writing in a foreign language at all.

TEACHING AND LEARNING STRATEGIES – SPECIAL SCHOOLS

In the special schools visited, classes were small but the teachers still tended to follow the same kind of lesson pattern as those in mainstream schools. In these special schools, however, the needs and limitations of individual pupils were known and catered for to a much greater degree. This may be partly because of the smaller numbers in a class but mostly because of the teacher's greater involvement with the class, not just as a language teacher.

Teachers explained that the needs of pupils in one type of special school would be different from those of pupils in other types of special school and how the teaching and learning strategies had to be adapted accordingly. In one EBD (Emotional and Behavioural Difficulties) school, for example, the teacher explained that the pupils in any one class would have been grouped together because of their special needs, which was appropriate, but it meant that she had a very mixed group as far as language learning was concerned. She thought it would be helpful if the groups could be separated out more:

> It would make it easier because, at the moment, you might have some kids who have done it for more than a year and they would find coming into the class that they might have done some of it elsewhere, so that would not be motivating for them. After all, our main rationale for doing it is to enhance their self-esteem, but if the kids have already experienced it, it could have the reverse effect and make them think that they are in a special school, doing the same old things that they have already done before.

Two special school teachers who worked in more than one institution explained that with all their classes they tried to get the pupils actively involved. As one said, 'You can't just stand in front of the class and get them to write things down, they like to do things physically.' Pupils would be asked to move around or manipulate cards or handle objects such as bottles and cans of drinks to be found in France. They also felt that though it was important to get pupils involved in understanding and joining in, this did not necessarily mean that they would have to speak much, or at all, in the foreign language:

> It is also good for kids who do not communicate much, who are not very verbal. It means that they do not necessarily have to say things them-selves. We also believe that kids have got the right to be silent. They can just receive things, they do not always have to respond.

In the EBD school referred to, the teacher explained that she did not usually get the pupils to work in pairs as they tended to be too disruptive. She preferred to have the whole class involved in active learning or individuals working on different things. On the other hand, in the MLD (Moderate Learning Difficulties) school where she also taught, she had larger groups and tended to teach the whole class together. A similar approach was adopted by a French teacher in a PH (Physical Handicapped) school:

> There are so few pupils in each class, they could have a computer each, and they could each be doing something different. But it's best if we are

all working in the same area because we can talk about it, have dialogues. I can spend time with whoever needs it.

Teachers in the SLD (Severe Learning Difficulties) schools visited stressed the need for the teaching to be appropriate, 'Although we welcome the input from the foreign language experts for ideas and techniques, here the techniques for SLD teachers are needed.' They felt it was important to make the language alive, to make it real, as one teacher described:

We try and make things as real as possible. For example, we use phone calls, real ones, from one room to another, so that the pupil has to say '*Bonjour*' and so on. We also try and use real foods rather than just pictures of foods.

One of the main points which emerged from the teachers in the special schools was the need to vary the activities even though the focus of what was being learned was very limited and did not change very much.

Children in the special schools were there because of their particular disabilities or learning difficulties, and therefore the range of achievement in terms of learning a foreign language could be quite broad. When asked how he differentiated between pupils of different levels of attainment, one teacher responded:

I probably expect more from some children than others. Sometimes I can split them into groups, it depends on how many staff you've got to manage the different groups. The main thing I find is to make the lessons enjoyable, doing games so that all can participate.

This approach of expecting different outcomes from different children was also used in a PH school, as the head described:

[the teacher] will deliver different oral challenges at different levels. For example, some pupils will only be required to recognise something; others will be required to listen and respond to quite complicated things and others will be required to listen to quite complicated things and respond in quite a complicated manner.

According to presentations made by special school teachers at a conference organised by CILT (Centre for Information on Language Teaching and Research), some schools were introducing the language across the curriculum, where this was possible. For example, in PE, the parts of the body would be identified in French, and in cookery, French food was discussed.

LEARNING ACTIVITIES AND MATERIALS

In the previous sections examples have been given of different approaches that can be adopted to try and ensure that pupils of all levels and particularly those with special needs experience success in foreign language learning. This section contains some more detailed suggestions for ways of making tasks and materials more accessible, drawn from the ideas of teachers of both languages and special needs. This does not represent any attempt to be comprehensive, but may provide some useful ideas or starting points for other teachers to develop tasks and materials of their own.

Topics

A modern language teacher in a mainstream school explained one of the ways he and his colleagues tried to cater for pupils who had poor retention and a short memory span:

> With more able pupils you tend to take a block-building approach; with the less able, we tend to teach in a more self-contained way. You can't rely on them having retained things from the last lesson, so one moves from one topic area to another without there necessarily being progression in terms of difficulty, but it's another area, and we are hoping that they will carry things through from one area to another.

A teacher in another school had reduced each topic into small sub-sections so that pupils only had to deal with a very limited range of vocabulary and structures for each sub-topic. In this way pupils could build up their knowledge gradually.

Reading

A lot of the work which teachers have carried out has been based around the production of materials which are clearly presented in terms of layout, style and content. In reading activities, for example, materials can be simplified so that each page only contains a limited number of words. Pupils can be asked to underline key words, phrases or sections rather than to answer questions of detail. Longer texts can be broken up through highlighting or boxing in relevant sections, or transferring sections onto separate cards.

The content and design of worksheets may also require further thought: a head of special needs pointed out that worksheets often had no instructions or ones which were too complex for some pupils. Some worksheets may also contain a mixture of English and target language words and phrases and pupils may be uncertain as to which language should be used for their responses. This teacher suggested that it would be better to use just one language on such sheets wherever possible.

Games and puzzles can be designed which require pupils to match cards with words or sentences on them, or cards which link pictures with written labels or captions. Pupils with sight problems may need pictures or words enlarged or perhaps, as a teacher in a PH school suggested, on different-coloured paper. It was also pointed out on the INSET course that some pupils cannot read capital letters, so texts should be in lower case, and typed rather than handwritten where this was possible. Pupils with no sight will need to be provided with as wide a range of braille materials as possible.

Listening and speaking

As far as listening and speaking activities are concerned, an approach suggested to make sure that all pupils are participating is to get them to note things down whilst the teacher or other pupils are speaking and perhaps read them back afterwards. This would not involve complex writing skills as a note of the numbers could be taken or the first letter only of words. For active listening activities in particular, pupils are encouraged to listen but are not obliged to respond in the foreign language, through the use of such tasks as:

- filling in gaps
- tracing the route on a map
- true/false questions
- listening for key vocabulary and ticking or crossing-off from pictures or a list as they are heard
- linking up drawings and vocabulary
- filling in a map
- note taking
- using the concept keyboard and other information technology.

The maps or grids supplied for pupils could provide different levels of support: for the low attainers, some of the gaps could be filled, or the vocabulary could be provided at the side, whereas for higher attainers all the gaps would be blank. Another way of differentiating the task in a listening activity would be for groups of pupils to work together; the higher attaining pupils would write the answers on a carbon sheet, once the group had agreed on the correct responses. At the end of the session, some pupils would keep the top copies, and others, who might have had difficulty doing the writing themselves, would have a written record of the responses on the carbon copies. Alternatively, different groups of pupils could be asked to listen out for different pieces of information, and at the end all the information would be pooled.

In a PH school visited, where classes learning a language were very small, the teacher recorded onto individual cassettes all the words, phrases and sentences that pupils were to practise and learn for homework. She described how she had attempted to do this when working in a mainstream school but because of the numbers involved it had been impossible to sustain. She found with her current pupils it enabled them all to practise at home, without embarrassment, and it provided pupils with the opportunity to replay the tape and repeat the words and phrases as often as necessary.

Language Master machines were used by teachers in some of the schools for pupils to practise listening to or repeating the words in the foreign language, as were individual headsets and cassette players.

With regard to pupils with impaired hearing, teachers suggested various strategies that could be adopted to help with listening activities. Such pupils need to be at the front of the class, facing the teacher, and the teacher needs to continue facing the pupils, so that they can lip read what is being said. It was pointed out by a special needs teacher that pupils do not always want to find themselves in the position of constantly asking the teacher to repeat things, so they needed the option of lip reading. A language teacher who will be teaching a boy with a hearing impairment next term described how she will try and support him: 'If they are in groups doing a listening exercise with headphones, I suppose what I will do is, I'll do it with him, speaking to him rather than him using the headphones.' In some schools, a support teacher might be available to help children with hearing difficulties by repeating what has been said by the class teacher.

Writing

Writing in the foreign language was perceived by many teachers in both mainstream and special schools as the most difficult skill for some pupils to acquire. It was considered not just difficult but inappropriate for some pupils, especially those with severe learning difficulties, to spend any time on it. In some cases, writing was rejected on the grounds that it had no relevance to the pupils' interests or future activities, in other cases it was seen as too difficult or laborious for pupils with physical or mental disabilities and would not give them much sense of achievement. As a nursing assistant in a PH school explained:

> In terms of writing, we don't do a lot of it, partly because for a lot of pupils it's very slow and we wouldn't want them to spend a great deal of time producing just one or two sentences. It wouldn't be very satisfying for them, so we do a lot of labelling and sticking things on walls, producing things from the computer.

The computer was seen as a useful tool in a number of ways. For example, for pupils with poor motor skills who find handwriting difficult, using the computer to write enabled them to concentrate on the content of the activity and at the end produce a beautifully presented printed piece of work. Concept keyboards have also been found useful for pupils who might have difficulty manipulating conventional keyboards. In one SLD school the head explained why touch screens were even more useful as they did not require users to shift their focus from the keyboard up to the screen. A wide range of software is now available, and by using both general and foreign language programmes teachers can produce a variety of activities for use at different levels. Both modern language teachers and special needs teachers have been developing their own materials for use on the computer, and work on concept keyboard overlays, in particular, is widespread.

SUMMARY

In this chapter it is suggested that teachers need to take account of their own teaching style and they need to consider carefully the content and design of activities and supporting materials. The main messages from the teachers can be summarised as follows:

- teachers should ensure that all pupils participate in oral work by making such activities sharply focused and of limited duration;
- pupils may gain more benefit from individual teaching or working in a small group than through participation in whole-class activities;
- instructions on procedures and activities should be kept short and, where possible, restricted to one language (either the target language or English, as appropriate) rather than a mixture;
- support teachers should be able to help both statemented pupils and others in the class who require extra attention;
- other pupils can successfully provide support to their classmates with learning difficulties;
- giving pupils more responsibility for their own learning facilitates teacher flexibility and may enhance pupil motivation;
- tasks and materials need to be differentiated according to the needs and abilities of the pupils;
- activities need to get pupils involved physically through speaking, moving, handling objects, using equipment, noting down answers.

Many of these approaches may be familiar to teachers with experience of teaching pupils with special needs, in small withdrawal groups or in special schools. The ease with which they can be adopted or developed by language teachers in mainstream schools, dealing with large mixed-attainment classes, may depend on the degree of support and training with which they are provided.

REFERENCES

Department of Education and Science Assessment of Performance Unit (1985) *Foreign Language Performance in Schools: Report on the 1983 surveys of French, German and Spanish*, London: DES.
Department of Education and Science Assessment of Performance Unit (1986) *Foreign Language Performance in Schools: Report on the 1984 survey of French*, London: DES.

Department of Education and Science and Welsh Office (1986) *Foreign Languages in the School Curriculum. A draft statement of policy*, London: HMSO.

Department of Education and Science Assessment of Performance Unit (1987) *Foreign Language Performance in Schools: Report on the 1985 survey of French*, London: HMSO.

Department of Education and Science: HMI (1987) *Modern Foreign Languages to 16*, London: HMSO.

Hegarty, S. and Pocklington, K. with Lucas, D. (1981) *Educating Pupils with Special Needs in the Ordinary School*, Windsor: NFER-Nelson.

Montgomery, D. (1990) *Children with Learning Difficulties*, London: Cassell.

Chapter 11

Learning, acquiring, remembering and producing language

Earl W. Stevick

LEARNING AND ACQUIRING

There are a few questions which have occupied language teachers for centuries and probably always will. Of these perhaps the most basic is 'How does a person come to control a language anyway?' We all achieved this feat with our first language, and many of us have gained some ability in other languages by studying them in school. The term 'acquisition' is sometimes used for the former, and 'learning' for what goes on in the classroom. There has been considerable discussion about whether these two processes are essentially the same, or essentially different. Until very recently, however, people have generally assumed that one followed the other with perhaps a few years' overlap. The ability to 'acquire' supposedly died out at about the age of puberty, while 'learning' became possible only in the early school years as the necessary 'readinesses' developed.

More recently, though, some research has indicated that the picture is not quite like that. It may be that the same kind of acquisition we see in children can continue well into adulthood – perhaps throughout life. Or it may be that what some people call 'adult acquisition' is really a third process. Be that as it may, however, it is becoming clear that adults and adolescents do have available to them at least two modes of gaining control of a new language.

The better known of these two modes is (in a special, narrowed sense) called 'learning'. Here, learning begins with selection of some clearly defined element which is to be learned. In helping someone else to learn, your job is to teach (again in a specially restricted sense of that word). In teaching, you first present the new item as clearly and interestingly as you can. Then you have your students practise the item in one way or another until they seem to have got it. When the time comes, you go on to test them on it. Finally, you may or may not get around to using it with them in some communicative way.

In this kind of teaching and learning, then, the very act of selecting an item pulls it out of the context of normal communicative exchange. To compensate for this severing of the normal interrelationship you may go to some length to provide context as you present, drill and test it.

In acquisition, the person who is doing the acquiring meets words in the full context of some kind of genuine human communication. There is no special presentation of a new item, no organised drilling, and no testing in the academic sense. Conversation is about things which the acquirer understands and which are already clear in his or her mind. Because a teacher cannot read minds, this requirement commonly means that in the beginning most of the conversation will be about what is present in the classroom at the time. The language used is generally at a level which the acquirer already controls *or a little beyond that level*. The acquirer follows the discourse comfortably, drawing on context to fill in the meanings of new words and constructions. In time he or she becomes able to produce new items correctly, but for a while may remain largely silent. When he or she does speak, those around him or her react in terms of their attempts to communicate, and not in terms of the correctness or incorrectness of what has been said.

This kind of acquisition takes time and patience. Until a student has acquired an item, he will make numerous errors in its use. Learning, by contrast, produces correct forms almost immediately.

There are however some weighty advantages to acquisition as compared with learning. What has been learned may be forgotten after (or before!) the next test, while what has been acquired is relatively permanent. What has been acquired serves directly as the basis for smooth production either of speech or of writing. Learned material is useful for monitoring, correcting or translating what has originated from material which has already been acquired either in the target language or in the native language, *but not for much else*. Not least, learning will work only for those items which can be stated fairly simply: English *house* corresponds to Spanish *casa*, for example, and the ending *-s* is used only for English verbs which are in the present tense with a third person singular subject. Acquisition works for everything: for all of the matters that I've just mentioned, but also for phonetic nuances, use of definite and indefinite articles, choice of just the right preposition or verb tense, and so on. The essential difference between learning and acquisition may lie in what the student does with what is put in front of him or her, but many parts of a language simply defy anyone to perform learning on them!

Over the centuries language teachers have used countless methods and techniques. Most of the time, by whatever method, we have concentrated on trying to teach so that our students would learn. Acquisition has come – when it has come at all – as a desirable but incidental by-product of good teaching and good learning. Its recent identification as a separate process casts light on what we have been doing all along. This knowledge also opens up exciting new prospects for what we may do in the future. Now that we see the difference between learning and acquisition, we can balance them against each other and combine them so that each will promote the other.

This, then, is a contrast which is worth exploring. Having said that, let's turn and look at one respect in which the two are special cases of a single phenomenon. That phenomenon is the storage and retrieval of memories.

REMEMBERING AND PRODUCING

In recent years there has been a great deal of fascinating research on human memory. One of the most basic facts which that research has brought to light is that what we think of as separate items are not stored separately. In talking with audiences about memory, I have many times asked people to call to mind some word which they have learned recently either in a foreign language or in their native language. Once they have identified such a word I ask them a series of questions: At what time of day did you learn it? Where were you? Which way were you facing? If you learned the word out of a book, where was it on the page? Was the type large, or small? If you learned the word from a person, where was that person? What general tone of voice did he or she use? What was the weather like? In general, people can come up with immediate and confident answers to questions such as these. *Sensory data that come together are stored together.*

Bringing back one item in an image also tends to bring back the other items in that same image. A well-known example of this principle is the power of odours to give vivid recollections of certain places or people: a whiff of coal smoke will always carry me back to Nashville in the mid-1950s, and lavender to the street corner in Yugoslavia where I once bought a vial of it. In the same way a couple may refer to a piece of music as 'our song' because it has the power to restore the sights and sensations of some time early in their courtship.

This does not mean that all items in a given image are equally clear and accessible, of course. We've all had the experience of remembering a face or a set of initials but not being able to come up with the name that goes with them. And going back to an earlier example, we know what it's like to see exactly where that grammatical rule was on the page, but not to be able to 'read' it. Nevertheless the other items in the image are there if only we could get at them.

A second basic fact about memory is related to this first one: *we can summon up two or more images, examine them, select items from each one, and form a new composite image that consists of parts of the old ones.* Again we find simple and well-known examples in our attempts to remember people's names: if I'm introduced to a man named O'Farrell, the name calls back an image which contains the name Farrell's – a chain of ice-cream restaurants in the area where I live. I picture this man entering one of these establishments, being surprised, and exclaiming 'Oh!' Then I store the new image in the hope that the next time I see his face it will bring the rest of the image back in a way that will enable me to call Mr O'Farrell by his name.

A third observation about these images (and then we will be ready to go back and look at learning and acquisition again): *every image contains auditory elements (if only silence), visual elements (if only darkness), emotional elements (if only boredom or indifference), tactile elements, olfactory elements, and elements representing the state of the body at the time the image was formed.* In any one image the items in, for example, the visual dimension may be many or few. Moreover, the various elements in a single image may be very closely integrated with one another. That is to say, they may fit together in such a way that a change in one would require a corresponding change in others. Or they may be merely juxtaposed with only a minimum of integration.

Images that come from outside the foreign-language classroom are almost always well integrated. This is not necessarily the case inside the language classroom, however. Take the cliché sentence 'The book is on the table.' If you are leaving the room just as I enter it and you know that I've come for a certain book, and if you want to be helpful, you may say exactly that sentence to me. Then your speaking it will be part of an image in which motive, physical situation and language are well integrated with one another. But suppose you say that sentence only because I have just said, 'The pen is on the table. Book.' Perhaps there's no book within sight at the time, or perhaps there is. It doesn't make any difference. You are responding only to my words – to one tiny segment of your sensory intake at the moment. You are also responding to two very non-specific motivations of your own – your desires to practice a pattern and to please me.

If in the same classroom instead of 'The pen is on the table. Book.' I had said 'We are here. Negative.' and you had responded with 'We are not here', the other elements in the total input image would have remained unchanged. This is an example of what I mean by an unintegrated image.

Sometimes we try to enrich an image and integrate it by using visual aids to illustrate what we have our students say: a book on the table one time, and a pen another time. This at least integrates a small part of the visual dimension with the linguistic dimension. But the motivational and social elements that would fit the words are still lacking. Even when we set up games in which students have to exchange or pool information which not all of them have, the motivational and social elements may still be of kinds which are seldom found outside the language classroom.

CONCLUSION

Now we are ready to take another look at learning and acquisition. It may be that both these processes are examples of what I have been saying about the storage, retrieval and reconstruction of images. The difference between them lies in the nature of the images. In acquisition the image from which we reconstruct what we are after is rich and well integrated, while in learning it is impoverished and unintegrated. The higher the quality of the image – that is, the richer and better integrated it is – the more easily we will be able to get back one part of it when we encounter another part. In addition, the affective side of what we acquire is usually of a kind which causes us to welcome the recall of an image. The affective side of some learning experiences is pleasant, but many of them contain heavy elements of feeling ignorant, powerless and constantly evaluated. When that is the case, a learned image may in some deep sense be unwelcome even at a time when our most obvious but more superficial motivations (the need to get a good grade or to sound educated, for example) make us try desperately to get it back.

If what I have said in the preceding paragraph is correct, then the modes of getting a new language which are available to a student are not exactly two in number. What we have been calling acquisition and learning now become only the ends of a continuum which rests on a single process. Both operate according to principles that are already familiar from research on memory. It seems to me that this conclusion throws light on both ends of that continuum without minimising the differences between them and without diminishing the urgent need to tell them apart and to exploit both of them.

The characteristic product of learning, then, is *fragments*. One serious limitation of learning is that those fragments do not support one another in the learner's mind the way the pieces of a completed jigsaw puzzle do. Instead they lie in the learner's mind like unassembled pieces of the puzzle of real communication, neatly stacked in little piles according to colour or size or other abstract criteria. So it is hardly surprising that what we have learned cannot serve us directly when we have something that we really want to say.

Wouldn't it be a good idea then to do away with learning altogether and concentrate our efforts on promoting acquisition? I don't think so. We've already seen that acquisition is a relatively slow process. In addition to that it may have its own characteristic product, which is not fragments but *fossils*. We all know people (perhaps we ourselves are such people!) who live for ten, twenty or more years in a foreign country conducting their daily affairs in the language of that country – who are, in other words, right in the middle of a genuine acquisition setting – but who persist in the same errors of pronunciation and grammar. Their competence in the language has 'fossilised' short of becoming identical with the competence of native speakers. If that can happen in life outside the classroom, how much sooner and how much more easily can it happen inside the classroom! Apparently people acquire as much of a language as they *really* need for what they *really* want, but only that much. One person really wants nothing to do with the foreign culture. That person will 'acquire' little or nothing. Another just wants to do necessary shopping and exchange a few simple greetings. Another wants to transact all his business with the native speakers fluently. Another is attracted to the culture and desires to become as much like the native speakers as possible. Given the same opportunities, each of these people will acquire a different amount of the language, but only the last is likely to carry the process to completion. Your success in helping people to acquire language in a classroom will therefore depend not only on the techniques you use, but also on how you, and what you do, affect their attitudes toward the language and the people who use it.

Learning and acquisition, then, are separate strands which you as teacher will wind together so that they supplement each other. Just how much you use of each will depend on your students. With some classes you will be able to discuss this matter openly with your students and then either work according to their preferences or work to change their preferences. In any case, you won't be able to wind the strands into a strong cable until you have seen the difference between them, and until your fingers have found out how to bend them and direct them.

The need to balance 'acquisition' and 'learning' against each other is not new to language teachers. We used to get at some of the same issues when we talked about the relationship between 'accuracy' and 'fluency'. When I was being trained, back in 1949, there was a clear rule: 'accuracy before fluency'. We assumed that a student's mind was like a clay tablet into which lines were being carved, one with each utterance, so as to produce the grooves, or 'linguistic competence', which would guide future performance. Any error, and particularly any uncorrected error, would contribute toward the wrong kind of groove, and so should be avoided.

Another assumption which lay behind the 'accuracy before fluency' maxim was that 'fluency' is simply the result of a large amount of practice. The formula was really an abbreviation for 'sufficient practice of accurate forms leads to the desired kind of fluency'.

Nowadays, we realise that the picture is not so simple as we used to think. For one thing, 'competence' is not two-dimensional like the grooves in a clay tablet, and what a learner practices is the mobilisation of competence, not just the repetition of performance. For another, fluency depends at least as much on emotional factors as on amount of practice, and too much insistence on accuracy can erode this essential foundation of fluency.

In summary, no one (I hope!) suggests that either accuracy or fluency be abandoned in favour of the other. The question about maintaining accuracy is not 'whether'; it is 'when' – and 'how'.

Chapter 12

Getting pupils talking

Iain Mitchell

We are all capable of speaking a foreign language – we all learnt English as children and that is one of the most difficult languages there is (*sic*).

(advertisement for a self-study language course)

The conditions in which we learnt our native tongue were, however, quite unique. We were surrounded by the language for some years before we actually started talking. Not wasted time, although it is difficult to quantify what was happening; we heard sounds, intonation, patterns – and we were making connections about meaning. We were not under pressure to start using language. None of us started talking before we wanted to – our parents could not force us to start.

There are obvious differences between a young child learning English as his or her mother tongue and that same person as an adolescent learning French at school. The underlying motivation cannot be there – as Eric Hawkins has said, if you have labelled the world once in your mother tongue, there seems to be little need to label it again in another:

> Much (not all) L2 learning is *re*-naming already known concepts (e.g. what is the French for the sun and the moon etc.). The excitement (motivation) of discovering a new concept is missing – the learner already knows the concept exists. The excitement of *learning a new name* for it is less compelling.

(Hawkins 1981)

The British classroom is not a 'natural' environment for the French language. The way languages have traditionally been taught is the opposite of what happened in our early lives. The teacher decides what the pupil needs to say and feeds the pupil appropriate language. The teacher, more omnipotent than the infant's parent, can make the learner speak (and in public) whether the learner is 'ready' or not.

Is it none the less possible, as language teachers, to take some steps to replicate some of the conditions of early life, to create a natural 'linguistic' environment and foster a real 'need' for pupils to use this new language to communicate, to speak when they themselves want to?

CREATING A LINGUISTIC ENVIRONMENT

Language teachers have always tried to simulate the linguistic environment of the country in question, by making their classrooms look and feel French or German, through displays, posters, and resources such as magazines and books. But we can also do it by making certain that the learners are immersed in the sounds of the language (just as infants they were surrounded by the mother tongue) without always knowing exactly how it is affecting them.

Using the target language

The teacher who conducts the whole lesson in the target language, demonstrates that the language can be an effective method of communicating any message. The teacher will use a whole variety of strategies to communicate – mime, signs, drawings, as well as linguistic devices such as repetition, paraphrase or selective use of cognates. Pupils grasp the message in different ways. When some pupils were to asked to reflect (in English) on how they understood what was being said to them during their lessons, they came up with the following: 'the teacher uses signs', 'we are doing something we have done before', 'the words sound like English', 'you listen for the words you know and work out the rest'; and 'we watch what everybody else is doing and do the same'.

The unpredictable

As well as this conscious and structured use of language there can be another more open and unpredictable layer of language from the teacher that perhaps comes closer to the variety the young child hears in its own language. The resourceful language teacher can bring in a whole range of language in an apparently random manner. In a lesson about daily routine, I observed one teacher talking quite specifically about what he had actually done that morning (getting up, shaving, breakfast, etc.) and then suddenly launching into a story about his going jogging in the country and seeing a fox for the first time. The story had not been planned as part of the lesson, but the telling of it was, almost subconsciously, carefully structured, and the personalised nature of the incident held the attention of the group. The narrative language was new for the pupils, the chance recounting of a chance event threw up a whole range of language, some known and some new. They were under no pressure other than to 'enjoy' the story. Morgan and Rinvolucri (1983) stress the importance of this type of language:

[the language is] sometimes fluent, sometimes hesitant and uncertain, broken by irregular pauses, but always definitely spoken language, the language of personal communication that is so often absent from the foreign language classroom.

(Morgan and Rinvolucri 1983)

Chance happenings in the class however trivial, but none the less real, can enrich in unpredictable ways the pupils' linguistic world.

Other voices

The presence of another speaker, such as a language assistant, greatly enhances what the pupils experience. The same words and phrases can be heard, in echo, from two different voices, providing immediate reinforcement. The range of language may be similar to when the teacher is working alone, but the context will have changed. Instead of monologues, the pupil now hears conversations and dialogues. The conversation on occasions may not be directed at the pupils (but this in itself can be a motivator to try to understand the message). This conversational language does not have to be limited to the assistant – many language departments have a policy of teachers talking to each other in the target language when in the presence of pupils. Any native speaker visitors to the languages classroom can also be exploited. These visitors will probably not use precisely the language the teacher might want them to use, but it can be important in helping the pupils gain confidence in coping with the very unexpected nature of such encounters.

Good language lessons will often include taped material, either video or audio, and most teachers now have regular use of a tape-recorder and, at least on an occasional basis, video. The value of access to such a variety of native voices should not be underestimated. It may sometimes be felt that a tape is too difficult, that the speakers are talking too fast, or that they have a difficult accent. The national curriculum states (in the Programme of Study for Understanding and Responding) that, 'pupils should have regular opportunities to . . . listen attentively' (DES 1991). Types of tasks to encourage pupils to 'listen attentively' to fast, not easily comprehensible language may be, in linguistic terms, very simple. For example, from a tape of different travellers on the Paris métro asking the way to their destinations, the teacher may only be asking the pupils to identify from a list or map the order in which certain stations are mentioned. In essence the task is no more than sorting the order in which certain words are heard, but the real reason for listening to the tape is to allow the pupils to hear a variety of native voices talking without putting them under pressure to do something too demanding with the material in linguistic terms. (This would probably not be the only task you would set but it would make certain that pupils, as a minimum exercise, listen to all of the tape.) The experience is similar to that of the young child listening to his or her parents – for whatever reason, there will be a focus on the language without any requirement to respond linguistically.

GETTING THE PUPILS TALKING

No matter how rich this linguistic 'environment' can be, it would be unrealistic for the language teacher to sit back and wait until the pupils 'feel the need' to begin to express themselves. None the less the variety and the richness of the language that the pupils are being exposed to can, with careful guidance from the teacher, encourage the pupils to start using language for their own purposes.

Creating a structure

Just as there are fixed points in a lesson when the teacher will say certain things – '*Ouvrez vos cahiers; Écoutez la cassette; Allez-vous-en!*' – there are fixed points in a lesson where the pupils can themselves make contributions in the target language. Before the lesson begins they can tell the teacher who, is absent – '*Paul n'est pas là*'; if they have a problem – '*j'ai oublié mes devoirs*'; when they have finished a piece of work – '*j'ai fini*'. The pupils can make these statements without prompting from the teacher – they them-selves come to recognise the appropriateness of them at that moment. The range of such possible statements is probably fairly predictable, and lan-guage departments would often agree on a list of phrases to be introduced during Year 7, whenever the pupils find they need them. This language can evolve: '*j'ai fini*' can become '*je n'ai pas fini*', '*j'ai presque fini*', '*nous avons fini*'; '*Paul n'est pas là*' to '*je n'étais pas là – j'étais en vacances*'. The teacher may have a structure in mind – extending the pupils' awareness of, for example, different grammatical constructions long before they are 'formally' introduced. These phrases can be recorded and can be seen as an evolving list. The language can be recognised as important language, as central to what is being learnt as the language of the coursebook.

This use of language by the pupils can be planned for by the department; it is predictable and the need for it is highlighted by the teacher. There can be another level for pupils to operate on. It is much more personal and much less easy to predict.

The pupils' own needs

Stevick, talking about the difference between learning (as happens in the languages classroom) and acquisition (as normally happens in one's mother tongue), makes the point:

In acquisition, the person who is doing the acquiring meets words in the full context of some kind of genuine human communication. There is no special presentation of a new item, no organised drilling, no testing in the academic sense. Conversation is about things that the acquirer understands and which are already clear in his mind.

(Stevick 1982)

The way pupils try to express themselves when they have a real, important message to communicate may appear to be haphazard, ungrammatical and even contain some English: '*Monsieur, la chaise est malade*'/'*Kann ich geben die Hefts?*'

There is a natural desire on the part of the teacher to want to correct immediately but it can be more useful to respond by reacting to the meaning of the statement: '*Alors il y a une autre chaise là-bas qui n'est pas cassée*'/ '*Nein, ich will die Hefte ausgeben.*' It may be that the response contains a form of correction (*cassée/Hefte*) but it is subsumed in the message. In the short term it is best to leave it at that, but at an appropriate point, such as the end of the lesson, to refer the whole class back to the interchange and ask them to add a version of that statement to their list: '*Rappelez-vous que Natalie avait un problème avec sa chaise. Si vous avez un problème comme ça avec votre chaise vous pouvez dire "Ma chaise est cassée" – alors notez ça!*'

This might seem like a dead hand on an ephemeral passing conversation – however, done at a reasonable distance in time (enough for the individual still to be able to remember the occasion), it allows the teacher to do any necessary 'improving' to the language without loss of face for the pupil, and emphasises the importance the teacher puts on pupils' thinking through ways of trying to get their message across.

Phrases amassed in this way can illustrate a wide diversity of syntax, a variety of statements and questions that have come from the pupils' own needs. Thus with a Year 7 class, a 'list' one year might include: *j'ai été à l'hôpital; je ne veux pas; je crois que ma lettre est à la maison; j'ai mal au doigt;* but next year be quite different. Pupils can be encouraged to use the language wherever possible, to experiment and change it to fit new contexts. If the same pupil, at a later date, said to the teacher, for example, '*Mon stylo est malade*', the teacher might feign incomprehension – '*Malade, quoi? A l'hôpital?*' – and encourage the pupil to check for the required language, on the list or with other pupils. Some pupils will remember more language than others but it is noticeable that all pupils can 'adopt' certain pieces of language – all will know at least some of the phrases.

The teacher may also suggest that a simplified form of a phrase can easily be used in other contexts – for example, *J'ai un problème avec ma table/avec les devoirs/avec Stephen* – but it is important to feed pupils a good variety of specific and even on occasions unusual language. This language, together with the stock language of the classroom (*j'ai fini; j'ai oublié mon cahier*) is organic – the more the pupils know the more they will want to experiment.

There will still be those pupils who may feel under pressure to perform before they have decided they are ready. Privacy should be appreciated and pupils encouraged to talk to the teacher on a one-to-one basis. In one Year 8 lesson recently observed, short private exchanges with the teacher as the class was arriving included someone who had lost all his books, someone who hoped that the class would watch television during the lesson, and someone who had telephoned her penfriend in Germany the night before. A stratagem used by some teachers, on a totally subjective basis, is to award points to pupils who say anything unexpected and good (in the teacher's or other pupils' opinion) during the lesson. This can be justified as it can kick start the pupils into a free and quite experimental use of language. Once the pupils get into the habit of expressing themselves in the target language whenever they need to, they forget why they first decided to do it.

PUPILS TALKING TO EACH OTHER

Everything so far has directly involved the teacher and the pupil talking together. What are the chances that this will carry over into pupil–pupil interaction away from the direct control of the teacher? It is safe to say that it will not happen if the steps described above have not taken place. If the pupils have not heard countless examples of successful, real 'communication' in the public domain of the classroom, from the teacher and from other pupils, there will be no rationale for them to apply themselves to it on their own. The nature of tasks where the pupils are working independently of the teacher, particularly in the early days of language learning, needs to be carefully considered. Typical early oral tasks that involve pupil–pupil inter-action include pair work and class surveys.

Developing a pair work conversation

Pupils need a very clear idea of what language they are going to require to do the task (the model language for a task can be available for referral on the board). The pupils will need the security of knowing that they can complete the task effectively but with the rider that, 'you can say anything else you want to that you think is appropriate'.

In one example observed, pairs in a Year 7 class were interviewing each other about what they liked doing after school – they had a model conver-sation on the board but they were encouraged to develop this. Every few minutes they would swap partners. The aim was to consolidate the basic conversation, to work with different people and to experiment with ways of bringing in other language. (The words in italics are those they added themselves):

1 Qu'est-ce que tu fais après les cours?
2 Je joue au karate
1 Qu'est-ce que tu fais quelquefois?
2 Je regarde la télé
1 Qu'est-ce que tu ne fais jamais?
2 Je ne fais jamais les cours. *Les cours n'est pas bon. Karate est fantastique.*
   Ton ordinateur est bon?
1 *Oui! C'est super!*
2 *Quoi ordinateur tu as?*
1 *Nintendo*
2 *Oh, c'est très bon. Nintendo est très bon but très cher.*
1 *Oui*
2 *Je n'ai pas de ordinateur*
1 *Ah*
2 *Quoi games tu as pour Nintendo? Tu as (????)*
1 *Oui*
2 *C'est quoi – un, deux, trois?*
1 *Un*
2 *Oh, c'est excellent!*
1 *Oui*

The fact that the pupils were of differing levels of attainment was not a deterrent. The high-attaining pupil could be more resourceful in how to continue the conversation and developed strategies that the teacher had used in class (e.g. giving alternatives in a question). It was also clear that the pupils actually became more interested in the conversation when they struck out on their own – the language was not necessarily more complex, but it took on the feeling of a genuine interchange. The fact that they were changing partners every few minutes allowed them to experiment and develop their own ideas in the conversation.

Creating a new conversation

Alternatively pupils might be asked to incorporate different phrases from their list of 'useful phrases' but in a different context from normal. A group of Year 8 pupils were 'phoning' a take-away to order food and drink. Partners sat back to back with no eye contact and were forced to speak clearly and to 'repair' the conversation if they missed something. They had this time not been given specific language to include but all pupils used the basic 'survival' language of ordering food and drink. The new context and the fact that the pupils were used to using the language as the medium of communication resulted in a considerable range of other language being incorporated, including: *pardon, je n'ai pas compris; pardon j'ai oublié; oui c'est ça; c'est très cher; non c'est pas vrai; vite, vite; oui dans trente minutes.*

Such examples touch on the general tactics of conversation: repairing; supporting the other speaker; reacting to the unexpected. The actual language may be quite simple but more important is that the pupil understands that he or she is capable of using it.

Unstructured conversation

Occasionally it is even worth turning the task around and asking the pupils in groups of three or four to have a conversation in the target language about anything they like. Doing this, a Year 7 group were told that the only requirement was to keep the conversation going and to involve all members of the group. It was thus important for the more loquacious to find ways of including more reticent pupils. Observing what happened it was noticeable how many simple questions pupils could ask, the range of ways in which they could react, drawing in language from a variety of previously encountered contexts and creating new phrases – for example, combining two phrases to come up with '*Ah non, j'ai oublié c'est quoi en français!*'. Out of need they also used strategies to cope with not understanding the conversation, including repeating the problem word (*quoi? pardon? ordinateur?*).

That pupils will revert to their mother tongue when not under the teacher's direct supervision remains a considerable problem to which there is no one answer. All the strategies discussed above, both for listening and for speaking, can help create a confident atmosphere where the foreign language is seen as a natural way of communicating important messages. The teacher will also need to provide a range of supports that will encourage pupils to use the language. There can be constant reminders ('*Pas d'anglais dans la classe de français!*'), suggestions of technical phrases they may need for certain types of activities ('It's your turn; I've won; Give me' . . . etc.), and awarding points to any pupils heard talking to each other effectively in the target language.

The national curriculum for Modern Foreign Languages states as one of its key points that pupils should . . . 'acquire, learn and use the target language to communicate with each other, their teacher and other speakers of the language'. As well as the use of the target language by both pupils and teachers, the document emphasises the need for pupils to develop the ability to learn independently of the teacher, 'to work on their own and with others'. With careful planning, the 'alternative reality' we create in the languages classroom can combine with real needs to stimulate both teacher and learners.

REFERENCES

Department of Education and Science (1991) *Modern Foreign Languages in the National Curriculum*, London: HMSO.

Hawkins, E. (1981) *Modern Languages in the Curriculum*, Cambridge: Cambridge University Press.

Morgan, J. and M. Rinvolucri (1983) *Once Upon a Time*, Cambridge: Cambridge University Press.

Stevick, E. W. (1982) *Teaching and Learning Languages*, Cambridge: Cambridge University Press.

Chapter 13

Teaching grammar in the target language

Theodore B. Kalivoda

Conducting a class through sustained L2 (second language) use is a concept which provides for a major block of classroom time without oral L1 (first language) intervention. During this period, oral L2 is proposed for exclusive use to support goals for developing oral communicative skills. Frequent shifts by the teacher between L1 and L2 are seen to restrict opportunity for uninterrupted L2 listening, a phenomenon hypothesised to carry over to student oral production also, as it influences learners to disregard L2 when communicating in the classroom.

The nature of grammar learning is complex and under considerable debate. It is not clear how much learners need to be told about grammar nor how much practice they require. If the grammar presentation is highly detailed, especially on the beginning level, L1 is likely to be used, since its complexity defies comprehension in L2. It is likewise apt to be done in L1 if it requires students to verbalise rules, a questionable practice, since few students, according to Sharwood Smith, seem to be able to do it. If, on the other hand, the explanation is limited to a degree of explicitness which serves to introduce the grammar point, followed by induction-inducing practice, then communication might well be in L2.

A problem encountered in literature on grammar teaching is the absence of clear identification of the level of students being taught. A specialised context involving advanced learners who have little or no difficulty communicating in L2 but who would profit by instruction on refining their grammar skill must not be confused with students in developmental stages of communication. Much of the literature assumes an audience of learners presumed proficient in communication; hence it need not address the question of which language, L1 or L2, will be the vehicle for explanation. In such a situation, an L1/L2 mixture may be acceptable, since the learners can receive and discuss information in either language.

Such a scenario has no resemblance to that of schools in which massive numbers of students studying Spanish as a second language, including many in 'advanced' courses, are struggling to learn to communicate in Spanish. It is this scenario in which one must decide which language, L1 or L2, shall be the language of instruction. In order to make this decision, one must attend to identifying instructional goals which, for many teachers, will be directed toward developing commonly sought after communication skills, with considerable emphasis on listening and speaking. In conjunction with goal setting, it is crucial to deliberate on instructional processes, *vis-à-vis* the language of instruction, to provide for congruence between goals and processes.

A prime issue affecting these decisions is how much oral L2 use contributes to or interferes with goal attainment. Experimental evidence is minimal, especially in terms of L2 use in which caretaker speech and other psychological variables are built into the design. However, results of two studies by Seliger suggest a general guideline to the effect that 'using the target language as a tool for social interaction affects the rate of second language acquisition and the quality of second language acquisition' (262). Social interaction includes a variety of communicative situations in which genuine talk takes place. Information giving, a part of this process, could encompass grammar explanation.

Teachers, through practical experience, know what works in including grammar explanation in L2. Commonly used techniques are reflected in the concept of comprehensible input which utilises caretaker speech in the form of linguistic supports (e.g short utterances, simple vocabulary and syntax, repetitions) and extralinguistic supports (e.g. motor activity, use of visuals) (Kalivoda). Sharwood Smith (54), in his 'Type C' grammar manifestations, refers to the need for 'brief, indirect "clues"' as facilitating techniques. Rutherford (235) adds other possibilities such as the use of a 'contrast with a related structure or with selected ungrammaticality'.

An example of comprehensibility of grammar explanation in L2 might include visual markings on the blackboard (e.g. arrows, circling, underlining). In dealing with direct object pronouns one might find valuable the visual representation in Figure 13.1.

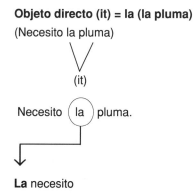

Figure 13.1 A visual representation for teaching direct object pronouns

The use of L1 (it), although miniscule, appears on the surface to be inconsistent with conducting the lesson in L2. It is, however, limited to writing and does not jeopardise the oral climate of the classroom. Also, initiating the instruction with a feminine singular example assumes that the instructor will continue a response pattern with the plural definite articles, masculine and feminine, converting them to direct objects (not necessarily all in the same lesson), which will later facilitate acquisition of *el* to *lo*. All of this, of course, is accompanied by practice on the grammar point in accord with learners' requirements.

Since more attention to explicit grammar may be needed and may be difficult if not impossible to do in L2, further grammar activity might be carried out in L1, but at a separate time identified as *L1-speaking time*. It is a time slot in which students may confirm and/or clarify their understanding through questions and discussions with the teacher. Discussion-provoking exercises of a problem-solving nature, both recognition and production types, might also be included. (Corder sees this latter activity as important for testing students' hypotheses about the grammar point under consideration and for combating errors made through overgeneralisation.)

The proposed L1 discussion time, perhaps of ten-minute duration at the end of the hour, is seen as totally separate from L2 use during the rest of the period so as not to interfere with sustained L2 listening and speaking opportunity. It may include discussion on other aspects of the lesson (e.g. culture) for which more in-depth understanding is desired. Figure 13.2 represents the separateness of L1 and L2 activities.

L2 (50 minutes)	L1 (10 minutes)
1. Limited grammar explanation followed by supporting practice 2. Other practice activities	1. Grammar discussion for confirming/clarifying understanding 2. Other discussion

Figure 13.2 L1 versus L2

I am suggesting a combined implicit (inductive) and explicit (deductive) approach to grammar teaching. Corder (133) also advances this dual strategy: 'What little we know about the psychological processes of second language learning, either from theory or from practical experience, suggests that a combination of induction and deduction produces the best results.' He sees this as a 'guided inductive' approach (133) because he deems learning as basically an inductive process but supported by explanation. Brown also values a combined approach. 'There is little value in raising the age-old debate over inductive versus deductive learning in a second language. It is hardly a question of "all or nothing"; some degree of both kinds of learning is clearly necessary' (267).

This combined approach to learning is not without its problems, since it can lead to serious erosion of oral L2 use in the classroom. Influenced by learning principles geared to deductive learning in general in the native language, foreign language teachers combine explanation in L1 with practice in L2. The approach may seem highly efficient in stimulating student discussion for maximising grammar knowledge, but is discussion via unbridled L1 use desirable given a foreign language class whose objectives prioritise performance over knowledge? In other words, what may be good for learning other subject matter in the students' native language may not be the best for learning a foreign language.

A general disregard for grammar teaching via L2 is seen in publications advancing activities that emphasise interest value at the expense of L2 use. This does not mean that interesting activities and L2 use are incompatible, but rather that the situation reflects a loss of perspective as to what the L2 class is all about. An activity in a current methods textbook encourages teachers to ask learners to 'explain how the negative sentences they just created are different from the affirmative ones' (Omaggio, 420). Assuming that students created the sentences orally, the ensuing student explanation, which must be done in L1 (given the L2 limitations of beginning students learning negation), misleadingly establishes as acceptable an environment in which L2 use can be relegated to exercise practice while L1 use is for communicative talk. Furthermore, both languages are freely mixed, denying a sustained L2 environment.

Another activity involves students practising the language while 'the teacher circulates to help and explain, based on individual needs. It is during this phase of the lesson that students who are still unsure about how the concept works can ask specific questions' (421). As in the first activity, discussion must take place in L1 since beginning students at the stage of being introduced to negative sentences are unable to ask questions in L2.

I am not suggesting that students' cognitive needs are unimportant, but rather that they be kept in perspective with the need for generous oral opportunity to use L2. Teacher talk in L1, often associated with grammar teaching, tends to produce explicit explanation, which in turn elicits a great deal of L1 talk from students. Likewise, classroom activities which elicit communication from students that is beyond their foreign language development contribute to widespread use of L1.

In place of an L1/L2 mix, an L2 sustained environment over most of the class hour, including grammar presentation, would seem to contribute to learners' oral language acquisition and to consistency with course goals of a communicative nature.

REFERENCES

Brown, H. Douglas. 1972. 'The Psychological Reality of "Grammar" in the ESL Classroom.' *TESOL Quarterly* 6: 263–69.

Chastain, Kenneth. 1987. 'Examining the Role of Grammar Explanation, Drills, and Exercises in the Development of Communication Skills.' *Hispania* 70: 160–66.

Corder, S. Pit. 1988. 'Pedagogic Grammars.' In William Rutherford, *et al.* (eds), *Grammar and Second Language Teaching*. New York: Newbury. 123–45.

Kalivoda, Theodore B. 1988. 'Teaching a Foreign Language Dominated Class.' *Hispania* 71: 954–58.

Omaggio, Alice C. 1986. *Teaching Language in Context*. Boston: Heinle & Heinle.

Rutherford, William and Michael Sharwood Smith (eds). 1988. *Grammar and Second Language Teaching*. New York: Newbury.

Rutherford, William. 1988. 'Functions of Grammar in a Language-Teaching Syllabus.' In William Rutherford, *et al.* (eds), *Grammar and Second Language Teaching*. New York: Newbury. 231–49.

Seliger, Herbert W. 1983. 'Learner Interaction in the Classroom and Its Effect on Language Acquisition.' In Herbert W. Seliger and Michael H. Long (eds), *Classroom Oriented Research in Second Language Acquisition*. Rowley, MA: Newbury. 246–66.

Sharwood Smith, Michael. 1988. 'Consciousness Raising and the Second Language Learner.' In William Rutherford, *et al.* (eds), *Grammar and Second Language Teaching*. New York: Newbury. 51–60.

Chapter 14

Why do I have to get it right anyway?

Brian Page

The difference between the old and the new objectives for foreign language teaching have always been neatly summed up for me in a parable published over twenty years ago (Corbett, 1965).

> The author recounts how, falling asleep after finishing marking his last GCE 'O' level translation paper one night, he dreams he is back in India where he served in the army. He is teaching English to two Indian soldiers. Suddenly there is commotion in the camp as it is learned that a dangerous tiger is about and also that the colonel's and the adjutant's ladies have gone into the jungle to pick flowers. They must be brought back quickly. The author seizes the opportunity and gives his two soldiers an Urdu sentence to translate and sends them off to look for the ladies. The sentence reads (in Urdu): '*Depart very quickly for an enormous tiger is approaching.*' A little later, one soldier reappears with an alarmed and breathless lady who is nevertheless unharmed. The second eventually arrives escorting the stretcher carrying the expiring remains of the other lady. How had the soldiers translated their sentences? The first lady reported that her soldier had said: '*You run quick big tiger he come.*' Using the GCE 'O' level marking scheme he had been applying before he fell asleep the author assessed it. 'This was clearly deplorable: −3 straight away for 'you run'; −2 for mood (indicative instead of imperative) and −1 for vocabulary (I might have accepted 'run away' or even 'run back', but 'run' alone was clearly inadmissible) . . . Next 'quick': . . . the scheme imposed a maximum deduction of 1 for any adverb. 'For' omitted −1; luckily for him I had not used 'since': the maximum deduction for a subordinating conjunction is 2 but for a coordinating conjunction only 1. 'Big' I thought inadequate for the Urdu word I had used: I wanted 'enormous', 'huge' or 'immense'; −1 therefore for vocabulary. −1 for 'he' as being superfluous, whether or not it was admissible as to gender. 'Come' was at least −2 for gross breach of concord . . . Total penalisation was therefore −9 and the mark for the sentence 1 out of 10.'

The second lady managed to express in her dying breath what the other soldier had said: *'Listen very carefully for a little bird is singing.'*

The author continues. 'This was a different matter. Syntactically it was perfect; there were, however, some errors of vocabulary – five in all – for which I had to make the appropriate deduction of one mark each. This soldier therefore scored 5 out of 10 and passed.'

The point the author was making in 1965 has been thoroughly accepted now, much to most people's relief. Grammar *per se* has been downgraded. It is now seen as serving the purpose of communication and not as existing as an independent self-justifying system. This argument, too, has always been accepted though with a slightly different slant. In 1954 the Modern Language Association published a pamphlet entitled *Grammar in relation to language learning*. In a section headed 'The necessity for accuracy in the study of languages in schools' it says: 'The study of grammatical accuracy and function . . . is indispensable for the achievement of a reasonable standard of accuracy in the use of language . . . Looseness in the use of language leads to loose thinking and robs the language of its capacity for precise expression.' It is clear that the authors see correct grammar as essential in making communications more exact. This is a common view still widely held. Yet it is obviously untrue. Grammatical accuracy is not always essential for accurate communication. Ungrammatical utterances do not always convey messages less accurately. Nor are they necessarily indicative of muddled thought. There is no 'loose thinking' or lack of 'precise expression' about: *'You run quick big tiger he come.'* It would be difficult to convey the message more succinctly, more urgently and more successfully. No English speaker hearing it would be in any doubt about the nature of the situation and the course of action that was being urged. It is this that modern examinations like GCSE recognise and that is why, at certain levels, full marks are awarded to such an utterance. It remains, however, that *'You run quick big tiger he come'* is wrong. No native English speaker would produce such an utterance except for comic effect. In that sense it is not English at all. But since we cannot condemn it in terms of 'practical communication' the objective of our language learning – on what grounds can we in fact condemn it? Are we to fall back on the position that we occupied before – you have to get it right because you have to get it right because that is how the language is? It seems a poor argument. What we must ask ourselves is, if correct grammar is not necessary for communication what is correct grammar for? What is the communicative value of correct grammar? The answer is clear. Correct grammar, like pronunciation, serves a social function. It tells the world something about what sort of person we are in the same way as our clothes, our lifestyle and the newspaper we read. We adopt the pronunciation and grammar of the group with which we wish to be identified. Most Scots always see themselves as Scots and therefore rarely lose their accents. Northerners, until comparatively recently, have often not had that confidence in their identity and, transposed into educated southern circles, frequently lose most of their accent. A taxi driver in an East End pub would not use the pronunciation and grammar of an Eton and Trinity senior civil servant unless he wished to invite ribald comment. Our use of language, including the accuracy of our grammar, invites interlocutors to regard us in a certain light and therefore to treat us in certain ways. Grammar does indeed have a communicative value but not necessarily in the transmission of the objective message. It transmits an image of the speaker. Most speakers wish to be accepted by their hearers so the use of correct grammar is mostly integrative in intent rather than instrumental. In foreign language learning the image projected by the learner to the native speaker can be a powerful motivator, particularly among adult learners. They are frequently the ones who want to get it 'right' because they don't want to appear foolish. Those whose professional self-image depends on accurate and elegant communi-cation (university academics are a good example) are frequently much more inhibited as language learners because they feel embarrassed at appearing diminished in the foreign language in an area essential to their being. The East End taxi driver is less so because his self-image depends on being a good taxi driver, a concept not endangered by his fractured French.

Degrees of embarrassment are, however, unlikely to yield a set of reliable assessment criteria. Interlocutor reaction will more readily produce useful definitions. If the learner speaks in certain ways what will the sympathetic native speaker think and what will be the effect on his or her linguistic behaviour? The answers could produce the criteria set out in Figure 14.1. It should be possible to refine them into an assessment instrument to judge foreign language production for GCSE. I should stress that these are a first attempt, have not been field-tested and are therefore imperfect and/or impractical in many ways. None the less, they do seem to me to present a way out of the current impasse. If we can set up an assessment instrument in this way we can talk to our learners about improving their grammar for communicative reasons. We can say: You should try to get your adjectives right and acquire as wide a vocabulary as possible because then you will communicate to your native speaker friend a much truer picture of yourself. She or he will be able to respond in a more natural manner and your relationship will be the richer and the more interesting. Or, if you find yourself working abroad, buying and selling for example, the impression you create on your potential customer or client will be that much more favourable.

REFERENCE

Corbett, R. (1965) 'No great matter', *Modern Languages* XLVI, 3.

In each case the informational content of the message is effectively conveyed.

1   Learner utterance: single or two-word utterances, strong interference from native pronunciation, considerable hesitation while searching for words, gesture, mime and illustrative sounds, e.g. *Bank here? Where station? No like.*

SNS likely reaction: single words spoken slowly and clearly while facing learner, much repetition and constant checking of understanding using words like *oui? compris?* Use of gesture, mime and illustrative sounds, etc.

2   Learner utterance: strings several words together but ungrammatically, heavily accented and very limited vocabulary, e.g. *Big tiger he come.*

SNS likely reaction: very simple sentences, slowly and clearly pronounced, use of mime and gesture.

3   Learner utterance: longer sentences, many well formed but most containing formal errors of some sort, few subordinate clauses or pronouns other than subject, a limited vocabulary which involves repetition and circumlocution to ensure communication, mispronunciations do not hinder communication but make the language distinctly non-standard.

SNS reaction: normal unhurried speech, some complex sentences, standard expressions, avoids slang and regionalisms.

4   Learner utterance: near native production, no conspicuous or consistent errors, wide range of vocabulary including some informal or slang expressions.

SNS reaction: almost natural speech, few allowances made, awareness that communication might break down if speed or amount of non-standard language is great.

Figure 14.1 Possible assessment criteria based on sympathetic native speaker reaction

Chapter 15

Raising reading attainment in modern languages

Paul McGowan and Maggie Turner

The work described in this chapter derives from a project specifically designed to raise reading attainment among Year 7 pupils (11–12-year-olds) in two Midlands secondary schools. The project was part of the LEA's response to the needs of ethnic minority pupils. It was offered to four departments in each school – Science, English, Geography and Modern Languages. Although reading is, *par excellence*, a cross-curricular issue, each area of the curriculum makes its own special demands on reading as a tool for learning. So, what pupils are to learn interacts in complex and unique ways with the place given to reading in the overall structure of the subject and the learning opportunities offered by the approach which teachers take. This article concentrates on the characteristics, issues and challenges to be faced in the teaching of Modern Languages to all pupils. The inclusion of a modern language in the curriculum of all pupils is a new departure for the subject, and one which is regarded with anxiety by some teachers. Nevertheless, other subjects have had to face similar challenges, and we would want to argue that they can be met, given an adequate theoretical and practical approach.

The ability to read well is a prerequisite to success at school. By 'success' we mean passing exams, at least up to GCSE level, and in those subjects considered prestigious and of an academic kind. Our assumption about what counts as success in school terms is allied to the belief that such achievements are within the reach of all but a tiny handful of pupils. That pupils do not currently achieve success in such numbers is to be explained largely, but not entirely, by reference to the goals set for them in school, our low expectations of them, and by our inadequate pedagogy. Research into school improvement, and the experience of educators, especially among black communities in the North American context, confirms that it is these aspects of schooling, and especially teacher expectations, which are the hardest to tackle.

At national level, concern about reading gives rise to periodic frenzies of alarm about (falling) standards – none of which have been matched by government funding of research into what would enable standards to rise.

There has actually been little extensive British research into reading in schools during the last ten years. Practitioners are forced to rely for guidance on such documents as *The Effective Use of Reading* (1978), *Extending Beginning Reading* (1981) and John Chapman's research on cohesion. There is a particular shortage of work on how pupils can best be helped to use reading for learning and independent study. Given the importance that GCSE has added to topic and project work, and the need for pupils to be properly prepared in Years 7–9 for the demands made by GCSE, there is indeed cause for concern about reading, but at the moment this concern is misdirected.

Such is the general context in which the discussion of reading development within modern languages must take place. However, to bring modern languages into the discussion at all is in itself an innovation, for it will be recognised on all sides that there has been little, if any, involvement of the subject in mainstream debates about language and learning. We shall not explore the reasons for this situation; we prefer to emphasise the desirability of establishing a dialogue between all interested parties, and to invite a commitment to a serious and sustained effort to achieve a common understanding of the issues.

But what are the issues which beset the profession where reading development is concerned, and in which we wish to see modern languages taking a full part? We list below just some of them, and raise some initial questions about how exactly they fit with the aims of teaching modern languages in this country.

1 Teachers' expectations

There is a strong sense that pupils should arrive at secondary school fully competent in all aspects of reading for learning. This is reflected in the training that most secondary teachers have received. There is an understanding that study skills are needed, but teachers have often not been shown how to develop their teaching repertoire in ways appropriate to their subject *and* to the development of reading within it.

There is an interesting contrast here for modern languages. First, it tends to be assumed that any reading that pupils will do in the early stages will be strictly controlled by the teacher, and will directly reflect the language they have been taught to use orally. Pupils are not expected to be able to cope with open-ended reading matter, and it is not expected that they should have been taught to do so, or that it is necessary to make such an assumption in order to proceed to the correct starting-point for the secondary programme. Second, there is an absence of specific content from modern languages, other than the structures and vocabulary of the course, which can easily become ends in themselves. That is, other than the language, there is no body of knowledge to be acquired from modern languages.

2 The importance of non-fiction

Children learn to read largely by reading fictional narrative. This in itself covers a multitude of genres, of course, but even so there develop certain features, such as the sense of a beginning, a middle and an end; the idea that some parts of the text can be safely skipped; that a personal involvement is invited; that you can look forward to being carried along by the action. Reading for learning in subjects is not like this, and pupils who transfer from narrative the expectation that it is may run into trouble and frustration.

Perhaps all that needs to be said at this stage, with reference to the role of reading in modern languages, is that there is no reason to think that it cannot support the development of a wider range of reading strategies.

3 More strategies

To read non-fiction, you have to be able to skim and scan, to pick out relevant information and discard the irrelevant, to go back over the same section time and again to get hold of the meaning, to relate the text to accompanying charts and diagrams, to synthesise information from one or more sources. To be able to do this requires a commitment on the part of the reader to the notion of study, which in turn requires a sense of accessibility and a challenge to be met.

The 'content-free' nature of modern languages, noted above, does not mean, of course, that it is not possible to attach it to an area of study derived from elsewhere in the curriculum or from the pupils' own interests, or both.

4 The retreat from print

This phrase was coined by the Effective Use of Reading Project (1978) to describe a response which they observed to be increasingly common in secondary schools. That is, a response to reading problems which produced fewer opportunities for pupils to develop the skills in which they were weak. The aim of the Project was therefore to convert what they saw as a vicious circle (pupils have problems reading–cut down the reading–pupils get worse at reading) into a virtuous circle: pupils have problems reading–do more reading–pupils read better.

Is it possible for pupils to read more than they do at the moment in modern languages?

5 The performance dip

With these points in mind, it is perhaps not surprising that it has been suggested that pupils' reading actually regresses, or at least marks time, after transfer from primary to secondary school. The evidence on this is not extensive, but it needs to be regarded as a serious possibility. The ILEA's Transfer Project found that the majority of pupils looked on the move to secondary school as an exciting opportunity, and that the prospect of 'harder work' inspired not fear and anxiety but a challenge that they were preparing to meet, and for which they believed they would be given the help they might need to overcome it.

This same Project found that although the opportunity to learn a foreign language was one of the things which children looked forward to, it was also a subject in which interest and motivation declined sharply during the first few terms after transfer.

6 Supportive strategies

The issue of developing a broader range of strategies for coping with a variety of text types cannot be divorced from the development of what the reader brings to the text in the form of prior knowledge of the subject. Opportunities for the reader to question what is written on the page are therefore needed. It cannot be simply a matter of practising specific techniques. Discussion with peers and with the teacher is an essential part of the learning process, as is an approach to learning which elicits from pupils what ideas they already have about the topic. This is important both to build confidence and also to indicate where misconceptions exist.

How are such considerations to be dealt with in the context of modern languages? How can the kinds of support for reading mentioned here be reconciled with an increased emphasis on the use of the target language in the classroom? To what extent do pupils' prior knowledge and learning matter to the planning and carrying out of modern languages courses?

7 Altering patterns of attainment

The rank order of pupils at the end of their secondary school career tends to be the same as it was at the start. (*The School Effect* [1989] noted this in relation to the relative positions of ethnic groups.) The gap between those who do better and those who do worse tends to widen. There is an air of inevitability about this process, but such a mood is not justified by the results of school improvement initiatives. In other words, schools can and sometimes do make a difference. Part of the explanation lies with a belief on the part of teachers that they do have the means and the opportunity to change the way things are.

In modern languages only a small number of pupils achieve grade A–C passes at GCSE. In the authority where the work reported here was carried out, it is about 13 per cent of the year group; nationally, the best authority manages around 30 per cent. Part of the development of a greater sense of efficacy in the teaching of modern languages, we would argue, has to do with rethinking the nature of language-learning processes, of which reading is one, in the light of insights from the research into reading acquisition and development. It also has to do with evolving practices for the classroom which are guided by such insights.

The issues which we are raising have been alluded to in the professional literature, but in sporadic fashion. O'Sullivan, for example, saw the situation in these terms:

- Modern language courses, encouraged by the demands of GCSE, have tended towards excessively narrow views of reading, i.e. an exclusive concentration on the 'practical' and 'realistic' (menus, shopping, short letters, etc.).
- There has been a concomitant absence of extensive reading material, opportunities or purposes.
- Although reading is acknowledged to be one of the key tools in the development of human consciousness and knowledge, it has no such role within modern languages.
- This distortion is caused largely by the dominant mode of thinking about how modern languages should be taught, in particular the role of teacher as 'dynamic presenter' and the division of language into 'active' and 'passive'.
- This latter point stems, in turn, from an outdated view of psycho-linguistics and human learning in general.

HMI issued their statement on modern languages in the 'Curriculum Matters' (DES 1987) series in the same year. In paragraph 42 of this document they say: 'The fact that pupils' reading ability is often at a higher level than their ability to speak or write the foreign language has clear implications for the level, complexity and authenticity of what they can be expected to read.'

This recognition of the asymmetrical development of reading and oracy is a crucial step towards a more adequate theory of modern language learning and it opens the way for some exciting developments of a very practical kind. But the implications mentioned by HMI in the above paragraph need to be clearly spelt out. In particular, it needs to be understood that when pupils begin their modern language course at the age of 11, they do not have to be taught all over again how to read.

This needs some emphasis, because when we look at the national curriculum statements of attainment for reading in modern languages, we find that throughout Levels 1 to 5, the development of reading is described principally in terms of word recognition and sentence complexity. From Level 6 to 10, the emphasis is principally on accessibility of content, variety of register and purposes for reading.

The assumption therefore continues to be that pupils can and should read only those snatches of language which they have been taught and have practised orally, and that reading activities akin to, and on a comparable level of maturity and interest to, those which pupils would be familiar with in their mother tongue can only begin once these basics have been learned. It is this kind of view of the reading process – this model of reading, if you like – which has led to the situation so trenchantly described by O'Sullivan above. Furthermore, it is a view of reading which is at variance with the one contained in the national curriculum for English. This is not, therefore, a solid basis for the development of the dialogue between all those who are concerned to promote pupils' reading skills.

However, we believe that the view of reading presented more generally within the national curriculum documents and the professional literature offers some potential for the development of ideas and practice. In addition to the remarks of O'Sullivan and HMI quoted earlier, the recent Working Party report observed: 'Pupils should have the opportunity to read as wide a variety of authentic texts as possible from the beginning of Key Stage 3' (para 5.19).

The same document also proposed a number of characteristics of good practice, among which were the following:

- activities are well matched to learners' ages and abilities (10.8)
- learners become increasingly independent in their work (10.14)
- some activities are planned in collaboration with other departments (10.16)
- learners read extensively for information and pleasure (10.17).

Working in this way, it is claimed, will allow pupils to handle the same types of topic as they would in their L1, bring their own knowledge and interests to bear on their learning, and engage them in activities which have a purpose beyond merely learning the language.

But how is it possible to talk, or even think, about giving pupils at the earliest stages of learning a foreign language materials which take no account of their novice status and which native speakers of the language would normally use? A degree of precision and modesty may be called for at this point. We need, first of all, to specify which languages we have in mind, and under what circumstances we are considering using the material. Second, none of the classroom activities under consideration can escape the normal requirements of good teaching – timing, pace, duration, preparation and so on. We are concerned with the development of good practice, not with gimmickry, fads or panaceas. So, the accessibility of texts will continue to relate to how well the teacher has prepared the pupils for what is to come.

One of the chief advantages, in terms of accessibility, with the main languages which are taught in our schools (French, German and Spanish) is the prevalence of linguistic and cultural elements which are cognate between these languages and English. By cognate in this sense we refer not only to

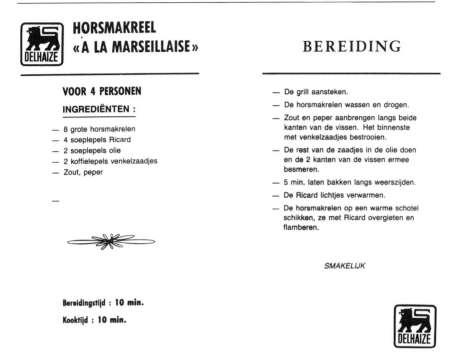

Figure 15.1 A text in Flemish

items of vocabulary, but more widely to sentence structure, discourse patterns, textual and cultural conventions.

As an illustration of just how powerful these relationships can be in aiding comprehension, try reading the Flemish text in Figure 15.1. We assume that most readers of this book have little familiarity with the language, and may therefore find themselves in a position akin to that of pupils at the start of their education in modern languages at age 11.

You may well have responded first and foremost to the format of the text, rather than elements within it. Once orientated to the general sense of what you are coping with, you will have recognised a good number of individual words on the basis of the fact that they are identical to English words in the same context. Other words you may have interpreted in the light of your knowledge of other languages. You will then probably have started to make reasonable guesses about those parts of the article that are not so amenable, using your general knowledge about cooking, if you have any. The more you have, the more you will have understood.

In other words, you have drawn on your existing knowledge of language and print conventions, on what you know generally about the world and about this area of activity in particular. Children in their first year of learning (say) French also possess such stores of knowledge. Is it possible for

TENNIS

Boris Becker devient
numéro un mondial

L'Allemand Boris Becker a rem-
porté le titre masculin des Interna-
tionaux d'Australie de tennis,
dimanche 27 janvier, à Melbourne.
En finale, le triple champion de
Wimbledon a battu en quatre sets
(1-6, 6-4, 6-4, 6-4) le Tchécoslo-
vaque Ivan Lendl, tête de série
numéro trois et vainqueur des
deux éditions précédentes. Becker,
vingt-trois ans, a enlevé ainsi son
cinquième titre du Grand Chelem.
Surtout, cette victoire lui a permis
de ravir la place de numéro un
mondial au Suédois Stefan Edberg,
ce qui était son objectif avoué
depuis deux ans.

Figure 15.2 Un championnat de tennis

them to utilise their knowledge to do similar things? Figures 15.2–15.5 show
some examples from the first-year classroom. The pupils are in their second
and third terms of learning French.

The choice of the article in Figure 15.2 was heavily determined by the
content of the course which the pupils were following. At the point where
we were working with them, they had reached a unit dealing with 'Likes and
Dislikes', in which leisure activities of various kinds were featured. The piece
was also topical, being drawn from the week's current news, carried by the
media both here and abroad. It had all of the features which we anticipated
would make it readily understandable to the pupils, and which we noted in
connection with the Flemish text. Pupils were encouraged to look for words
which were the same in French as in English, which were similar to English
words, and finally to make reasonable guesses about the meaning of other
words, given the context that they were building up, and what they might
already know about tennis in general, and this match in particular. As in all
areas of activity, some people know more than others, and sometimes the
pupil knows more than the teacher! After the pupils had worked in pairs, the
results were drawn together in a whole-class discussion, using an OHP
version of the original text, on which the teacher underlined the parts of the
text which had been understood. This is the version printed. Clearly, pupils
had derived the bulk of the meaning from the text in Figure 15.2 and had
done so under their own efforts, having been carefully prepared by the
teacher.

What we are doing here is making accessible to pupils reading material which is of a kind they would be expected to tackle in English, on the basis of prior knowledge of the subject; intrinsic interest and motivation; linguistic knowledge in general; topics made familiar by the language course. In other words, we are maximising the support provided by the context for reading in French, as we would do for any other successful reading activity in school.

SOS FANTOMES	UN FLIC A LA MATERNELLE
LE CHAUDRON NOIR	INDIANA JONES ET LA DERNIERE CROISADE
LA PETITE SIRENE	A LA POURSUITE D'OCTOBRE ROUGE
CHERI J'AI RETRECI LES GOSSES	
	MAMAN J'AI RATE L'AVION
ALLO MAMAN, ICI BEBE	LE MYSTERE VON BULOW

Figure 15.3 What are the titles in English of these recent films?

The example shown in Figure 15.3 also took place in the context of 'Likes and Dislikes'. Pupils again worked in pairs and then came together as a whole class to share ideas and suggestions about meanings. It should be pointed out that most of the films were current at the time, and that others were 'classics' in the world of young people's cinema. This produced the interesting result that, although most pupils were able to find the original titles even when they had not seen the film (they nevertheless knew all about it from friends who had or from reading about it in magazines), teachers unfamiliar with this world, but whose command of French was not in doubt, found difficulty with some of the less literal translations.

It was, in fact, possible to carry on a sophisticated discussion with the class about issues to do with translation and in the process to cover some points of grammar in a practical context. For example, that a literal correspondence sometimes exists between languages (*La Petite Sirène*); that sometimes word order alters slightly (*Le Chaudron noir*); that sometimes the source language has coined a new word which is not matched in the target language (*SOS Fantômes*); that sometimes there is not an equivalent phrase in the target language, but you can match the sense indirectly (*Allô maman, ici bébé*): and sometimes you may choose not to use a direct parallel, even though there is one available (*Maman j'ai raté l'avion*).

Actually, the pupils themselves were able to formulate most of these points themselves, in their own ways.

In the example shown in Figure 15.4, two pupils were asked to read the article together. There was no prior preparation, as we were interested to see

Incendie dans une maison près de Reims: six morts. – Six personnes d'une même famille sont mortes tôt, lundi matin 21 mai, dans l'incendie de leur maison dans le village de Loivre, près de Reims (Marne). L'incendie a éclaté, pour une raison encore inconnue, dans une maison individuelle d'un lotissement du village. Il a ravagé l'habitation, qui s'est ensuite écroulée. Les pompiers ont retiré des décombres les corps des deux parents, âgés de vingt-sept et vingt-huit ans, et de leurs quatre enfants, deux garçons et deux fillettes, âgés de trois à huit ans.

Figure 15.4 L'incendie d'une maison

on this occasion just how much pupils could get from a piece of authentic text, starting 'from scratch', as it were. They were told only that the report concerned a house fire. After their first reading, during which they were again encouraged to utilise clues from the range of cognate elements discussed earlier, and which they had already practised in other activities, the pupils volunteered the following observations about the text: that it concerned a family whose house had been burned down; it gave the location of the house and the date it had happened; the ages of the members of the family – parents and children; in addition, the children, two girls and two boys, were actually two sets of twins, and the house was either detached or semi-detached (they could not decide on this point). After a second reading, and in response to questions from the teacher, they added that the remains of the parents and children were found in the house, that the firemen had not arrived in time to save them, that the phrase '*six morts*' meant 'six victims' (a most appropriate choice of word for this particular style and register!) and that '*corps*' must mean 'bodies'. It should also be said that some of their ideas about the meaning of certain details were not so accurate, and that they were actually led astray in this by the very techniques which we were encouraging them to use. This is not to invalidate the techniques, however. For example, they took '*habitation*' to mean something like 'habit', and therefore concluded that a similar kind of incident had happened before! Thus, even when 'false cognates' crop up, the pupils were attempting to make appropriate sense, and to relate them to the general drift of the story.

The article in Figure 15.5 involved the same two pupils as the previous one. This time we were interested to see what effect the pupils' cultural knowledge would have on their ability to make sense of a text. One of the pupils was a Muslim, the other a Sikh. As it turned out, both showed great

Ramadan in France

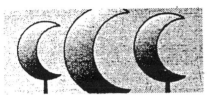

*I*L N'Y A pas de fête du printemps dans l'Islam. Pourtant, comme leurs ancêtres l'avaient fait bien avant la révélation du Coran à Mahomet (vers 610 de notre ère), la majorité des 3,5 millions de musulmans français observent le ramadan. Neuvième mois du calendrier islamique, c'est une période strictement religieuse, marquée par le **jeûne** et la prière. Ce mois est un mois sacré; pour cette raison, les musulmans donnent fréquemment le prénom de "Ramadan" aux jeunes garçons.

Quand commence-t-il? Avec la nouvelle lune, quand le **croissant** est visible à **l'oeil nu, selon** la tradition née au septième siècle en Arabie. Aujourd'hui encore c'est la règle, qui ne tient pas compte des variations de **fuseaux horaires** et qui implique donc que le ramadan ne commence pas le même jour aux deux extrémités du Maghreb, en Libye ou au Maroc.

En France, il a commencé cette année le 17 ou le 18 mars au matin. Dès **les premières lueurs de l'aube**, les musulmans cessent de manger et de boire et doivent consacrer leur journée à des activités de piété, de prières, de méditation et d'**aumônes**.

Pendant les 28 ou 29 jours du mois lunaire que dure le jeûne, le temps s'arrête — en théorie, du moins. La vie en France ne **se prête** pas facilement au respect de ce rythme ralenti. Il n'y a pas de fête pour marquer le début du jeûne; en revanche, il y en a une pour célébrer la fin du jeûne, **appelée al-Fitr**.

Ce jour-là les enfants et les femmes mettent leurs plus beaux habits.

Jadis, dans les pays du Maghreb (Algérie, Maroc, Tunisie) le travail agricole cessait, les maisons s'ouvraient aux **mendiants** qui étaient accueillis comme des membres de la famille. "C'était la fête de la joie et du partage, les enfants voulaient faire le jeûne pour entrer dans le monde des adultes, les parents devaient les freiner pour protéger leur croissance," se souvient Mohammed Arkoun, historien de l'Islam.

Aujourd'hui, les choses ont un peu changé. Selon quelques commentateurs, il est difficile de faire coïncider ces pratiques religieuses avec la vie moderne. Au Maghreb comme en France, les portes s'ouvrent moins vite aux pauvres à la fin du ramadan.

"Le ramadan, comme les cinq prières quotidiennes et le **pèlerinage à la Mecque**, se faisait de manière naturelle, sans contrainte. Aujourd'hui, beaucoup le font sous la **pression de l'entourage**, les rituels observés n'ont plus exactement le même sens," dit Mohammed Arkoun.

Glossaire/Glossary

un jeûne a fast
un croissant crescent (of the moon)
l'oeil nu (m) the naked eye
selon according to
un fuseau horaire time zone
les premières lueurs de l'aube the first sight of dawn
l'aumône (f) charity, alms
se prêter à to lend (oneself) to
jadis formerly
un mendiant beggar
un pèlerinage pilgrimage
la Mecque Mecca
la pression de l'entourage peer pressure

Figure 15.5 Ramadan: using pupils' cultural knowledge

Source: Education Guardian, 26 March 1991

interest in the subject matter, but the Muslim pupil took the lead in discussion and spoke with authority on related issues. As in the previous example, they were asked to look at the text without prior preparation. When asked what they had got from it, they mentioned: when Ramadan starts and ends; how many days it lasts; which month of the Islamic calendar it is; that it is a tradition for Libya, Morocco, Arabia; how it is celebrated in France. In discussion with the teacher, further issues were raised: the phrase 'c'est une période strictement religieuse' had caught the attention of the Muslim pupil, who went on to endorse the sentiment and stress the importance of it; great surprise was expressed by both pupils at the number of Muslims (which they read as 3 to 5 million) in France, which they had always assumed (and had perhaps been led to believe by their course materials) to be an all-white society. They had also picked up the idea that the French approach to Ramadan was more 'modern' than the UK's. Unfortunately, the teacher did not explore what they meant by this, but it is possible that they had spotted something in the second half of the text which could have given that impression.

One major possibility which we have not yet explored is the extent to which collaboration between modern languages and other curriculum areas can be harnessed to develop reading. Although the activity would be difficult to illustrate here, we have used a programme from the Channel 4 series *Eurocops*, in which we have combined the videotape of the programme (without subtitles), providing a transcript of the dialogue, and have devised activities in which pupils go between the different media in order to make the most effective use of all sources of input. An even more sophisticated use of the same, or similar, materials could be devised if the modern languages department were to team up with the English department – both departments concentrating on complementary aspects and activities. For example, the English department might concentrate on discussions (in English – and at a suitable level of sophistication) about characterisation and motive, plot development and so on. The modern languages interest could be in establishing the basic story.

Further opportunities for collaboration between departments could arise, for example in Geography. We were unfortunately unable to try out some ideas in this area, but it was intriguing that at the time we were working with the two schools, the French newspaper *Libération* published an article about the latest theories in the realm of plate tectonics, and accompanied its article with a diagram. This diagram would, in fact, have been very familiar to pupils, since they had just been studying the topic in their Geography course, and had actually been using similar material themselves! They would therefore have brought a good deal of prior knowledge to the French version, as an aid to their understanding of it.

When we start to look at the opportunities in these sorts of ways, it becomes clear that the possibilities are only just beginning to open up.

However, as the arguments of this article have tried to show, we will not find a way forward in practical terms until we have clarified our ideas at the theoretical level, to some extent at least. The direction is not all one way, of course. We have to try things out in practice, and then adjust our thinking if need be.

The starting-point, though, is that changes in the way reading is conceptualised may be needed if there is to be progress made by pupils in particular areas of the curriculum. It is not simply a matter of helping pupils to gain access to what is being offered. What is being offered and the form in which it is offered, may have to be altered. If our model of reading is inadequate, then we will be unable to assess pupils' real abilities, needs and progress, because we will be unable to see what they are doing and why they are doing it. However, the challenges and problems, as well as the opportunities, presented by each area of the curriculum must be clearly acknowledged. The requirements imposed by each area must not be swept aside in the name of 'cross-curricular skills'. What reading is must be fully worked out in the context of each area.

REFERENCES

Chapman, J. (1987) *Reading From 5–11 Years*, Open University Press.

Department of Education and Science (1987) *Modern Foreign Languages to 16. Curriculum Matters 8*. London, HMSO.

ILEA (1986) *ILEA Transfer Project*, ILEA Research and Statistics Branch.

Lunzer, E.A. and Gardner, K. (1978) *The Effective Use of Reading*, Schools Council/Heinemann.

O'Sullivan, T. (1987) 'Some thoughts on extensive reading in GCSE Modern Languages', *British Journal of Language Teaching* 25(5).

Smith, D. and Tomlinson, S. (1989) *The School Effect*, London, PS.

Southgate, V. *et al.* (1981) *Extending Beginning Reading*, Heinemann.

Part IV

Un second souffle

Injecting creativity into the language classroom

Chapter 16

A la recherche du stylo perdu

Ann Swarbrick

Narrow interpretations of the words 'communicative methodology' have often set foreign language learning in a utilitarian world. In our attempt to link classroom interaction with the 'real' world outside the classroom, we have reduced that reality to a world of tourism where many loaves are bought and many predictable transactions take place but where no one tells a joke or a story. The national curriculum requires teachers to create opportunities for pupils to express themselves creatively in the foreign language. This chapter attempts to underline the importance of this area of pupil thought, to suggest the conditions necessary to encourage it and to outline the steps teachers need to take in order to set up these opportunities. It takes as its focus creative writing though, as discussed below, writing is not a skill discrete unto itself but is influenced by what one hears, reads, smells, touches and sees. The chapter concludes with a concentration on one particular area of creative writing – poetry. It describes a poetry writing project during which pupils from twenty-five schools wrote poetry in five languages.

One of the most misleading assumptions made during the ascendancy of communicative methodology is that communication means only oral communication. A positive result of this assumption has been a much needed rise in the importance of talk in the foreign language classroom. The pendulum has swung away from writing as the most important skill and toward speaking and listening. But the result has been a retreat from anything seen as not directly encouraging the oral skill. The casualties have been reading and writing. Unless the balance is redressed soon, the criticism directed at us by future generations will reflect not an inability to speak a foreign language, as was the case pre-GCSE, but an inability to read or write it. Concentration on oral skills at the expense of others is both misguided and artificial since all of the skills are integral to and serve each other:

> There is . . . no more pernicious misunderstanding than to suppose that minutes spent on one skill are just so many minutes taken away from progress in the other three. Just as oral practice and discussion may

greatly improve the accuracy and coherence of what one writes, so writing may have a beneficial effect on one's oral production.

(Wringe 1989)

Nevertheless writing remains the most problematic of the skills in which to gain competence, for both teachers and pupils. Much of what is written is done to provide the teacher with a record that work has been covered. It is not an activity in its own right but one which 'services' (Rivers 1968) the other skills. So exercise books become full of labelled drawings – like illustrated dictionaries – or unconnected lists of words, or answers without questions which, once complete, serve no purpose for future reference or interest. Writing, then, has been relegated to the bottom of the league of skills. The argument for keeping it there runs like this: 'Most pupils find writing in a foreign language difficult, they will rarely need to write in adult life, so cut down on the amount of writing.' (The scenario is the same as that described by Paul McGowan and Maggie Turner in their chapter on reading earlier in this book, where they describe 'the retreat from print' (Chapter 15). Yet despite the fact that it is acknowledged that writing is a difficult skill for many pupils to acquire, it is often used as a convenient, though often inappropriate, means of assessing the other skills. In terms of assessment, as Rivers pointed out twenty-five years ago, teachers are often harshest on pupils in writing activities, the testimony for this being red-ink-spattered exercise books. Where an amount of free expression and experimentation is allowed in the spoken language, maybe because of the concrete evidence it produces, little freedom is allowed in writing. I do not offer this as an argument against assessing pupils' written work but as an argument for looking more closely at whether writing skills should be taught, and how and whether it should be acknowledged that an insistence on complete written accuracy is unrealistic and destructive to pupils' creative output.

Rivers describes five stages of development which pupils need to go through in acquiring competence in writing: copying, reproduction, recombination, guided writing and free writing. Attainment target 4 of the national curriculum recommends exactly this progression. Pupils should not be abandoned too early in their development as linguists to 'attempt a standard of expression beyond their state of knowledge' (Rivers 1968), but if they are allowed some freedom to write what they want to write, then writing becomes an enjoyable experience and will be seen as an act of communication even if what is written is only a short message on a Valentine card or whatever. Some learners learn better by writing things down. They use writing as a form of support when learning something new. This should not be discouraged (nor particularly encouraged, since production of incorrect forms of the written word may lead to later confusion), but we should move away from the assumption that everything written is for public consumption.

THE PURPOSE OF WRITING

> Pupils are motivated to write effectively when they can relate to the purpose of the piece of writing.
>
> (Woods 1986)

I can identify four reasons for writing:

- to give or respond to information
- to record a piece of information
- to give pleasure to another reader or oneself
- to express an idea or feeling one finds difficult to articulate.

Writing activities set in MFL classrooms in the last decade have concentrated on the first two of these reasons at the expense of the others. It is time to redress the balance, and the rest of this chapter will suggest ways of doing this.

Creative writing requires the learner to invest something of him- or herself in the activity. This may be in the creation of a poem or a story but equally it could be a piece of guided writing, for example a letter to a penfriend. If the learner is working from a model letter provided by the teacher but decides to adapt it in order to say something extra of the learner's own volition, then this may be regarded as a creative act. A creative writing task requires the learner to use the language that he or she has learnt or acquired in a less directed way than a drill or textbook exercise might require, to experiment with the language in order to express an idea and to adapt the same phrases to different contexts. A creative writing task might require the learner to write something that could be used in or out of the classroom, such as a questionnaire, a survey, a quiz or a game. Other forms of writing which lend themselves to creative output are: messages, diaries, invitations, graffiti, song lyrics, problem page letters, ransom notes, captions for strip cartoons, short stories, reviews, accounts of events, newspaper articles and poems (the list is not exhaustive).

One of the most motivating elements of creative writing is the presence of the reader. Teachers do well to provide an audience apart from themselves for their learners. Readers range from the foreign language assistant to a parallel class in the target country, to another class in the school, to a class in a school up the road, to a feeder primary class, to members of the wider school community. The learner's motivation to write is heightened because of the interest of the other party. This point does not refer exclusively to high-attaining pupils. Often low-attaining pupils lack the inhibitions of their peers who dwell on accuracy to a point where inhibition blocks creativity. This is not to say that producing a piece of writing with a reader in mind does not require extra care and redrafting but I shall return to this later.

CREATING THE CONDITIONS NECESSARY FOR CREATIVITY

The creative world is a sensitive place. Conditions might favourably or unfavourably affect the writer. This needs to be considered carefully since our attitude to tasks and to pupils might influence the quality of the output. Ruth Strang (1959) identified some destructive and constructive influences in the classroom. Destructive influences are: teacher indifference, the teacher's over-zealous desire to influence the outcome after which the learner feels the resultant work is more the teacher's work than hers, negative criticism, an unruly environment, lack of time, lack of adequate preparation for the task and unfamiliarity with the type of task. Constructive influences might be the converse of all of the above points but also praise where it is due, an atmosphere in which pupils are encouraged to share ideas and to show independence, mutual respect for creative ideas, pupils' ability to work co-operatively and collaboratively, a non-judgemental approach where the teacher is seen as adviser rather than judge, and a stimulus which provides a need and a reason to write. It is useful for learners to see the teacher as, in some ways, a creative model able and willing to do any activity set for pupils. So, if the activity is about producing a class poem, then the teacher might produce a model poem. Though conditions for creativity must be considered, it cannot be assumed that, if these are right, learners will automatically be able to respond to the task in silvery prose. Few people have this talent in their mother tongue; it would be unrealistic to make assumptions about capability in a foreign language. The process is as important as the end result:

> the amount of language learners have at their disposal for writing will be very limited. . . . At the same time the learners being more mature than they were when they learned to write in their mother tongue are conscious of the limitations which the foreign language imposes on the expression of their ideas. To resolve this problem it will be necessary to strike some sort of balance which prevents them from going beyond their linguistic attainment in the foreign language and yet will still provide them with writing activities which satisfy them on an intellectual level.
>
> (Byrne 1988: 6)

It is also necessary to warn that pupils unused to having their powers of imagination encouraged in the MFL classroom may take time to adjust. Teachers need to persevere not only in terms of encouraging pupils but also in terms of putting their own creative energy into devising different ways of stimulating pupils' creativity.

Pupils do not have the facility to pluck language from the air as they might in their mother tongue. As in the learning of any aspect of the language programme, they must get the language from somewhere. The teacher is an obvious source, but creative activities should not be seen as separate from other activities. So, in the same way as it is true that we must conduct lessons in the target language if we want pupils to be able to speak the language, so production in the written language is dependent on exactly the same oral input. Pupils must be exposed to language if they are to acquire it. Once they have acquired it, decoding it into the written word becomes less of a problem and less of an exercise in translating word for word. Iain Mitchell, earlier in this book (p. 114), describes the 'alternative reality' which is created in the language classroom when all business is conducted in the foreign language. This is essential if pupils are to get a feel for experimenting with language and making it their own. It is only with this amount of input that pupils will hear enough language to be confident to produce creative pieces of writing. To illustrate the point, this poem was written by a Year 7 boy after two terms of learning German:

'Meine besten Ausreden'
Entschuldigen Sie bitte!
Ich habe mein Lineal gegessen!
Ich habe keine Federmappe!
Mein Kopf schmerzt!
Meine Maus, Rex, ist tot!
Ich war nicht da, ich war in Deutschland!
Ich habe keine Ausreden!
Glauben Sie mir?

'My Best Excuses'
Excuse me please!
I have eaten my ruler!
I haven't got a pencil case!
My head hurts!
My mouse, Rex, is dead!
I was not there, I was in Germany!
I haven't got an excuse!
Do you believe me?

(Lee Moulds Ernulf Community School)

The boy produced the poem then asked for help with spelling but the source for much of his language is evidently habitual classroom language.

Another important element in developing pupils' creative skills is reading. Learners need to be familiar with a variety of written forms if they are to understand the power of the written word. If, for instance, the task is to write a story with a moral, they will approach this with much more confidence if they have read a variety of such stories in the foreign language. A creative teacher would seize such an opportunity to integrate the skills in this instance. Reading, writing and telling stories, though all requiring separate skills, can offer more scope to the imagination of the learner than discrete skill tasks. Little, Devitt and Singleton (1989) argue strongly that authentic texts provide what they call an 'acquisition-rich environment' and therefore should be a primary source of input in any foreign language teaching programme.

ENCOURAGING WRITTEN PRODUCTION

Group work in MFL has been much encouraged in recent years not least because it gives pupils a sense of security. They have the support of their peers in the activities they do and a small forum for discussion which is less daunting than the whole class. Discussing creative writing activities is important for the generation of ideas and for the facility of peer group assessment that it provides. The group might act as a form of quality control before the work is presented either to the teacher or to the rest of the class, or to whoever the reader might be. Individual work should not be abandoned totally, however. Group work can have a detrimental effect on some learners' creative output and an unremitting diet of any one form of grouping might affect motivation. Writing *with* pupils in the early stages of their learning can be a confidence enhancing strategy. If, for example, the class has been presented with an oral account of a series of events, they might feed back the language to the teacher to write up on the board or overhead projector in the form of a newspaper article. This provides the opportunity for pupils to see the spoken word decoded into the written word. It also invites discussion of alternatives since different pupils will suggest different language and perhaps a differing order of events. The teacher seen writing on the board or overhead projector to the instructions of the class in this way also demonstrates that the teacher has not made all of the decisions prior to the activity and that pupils have some say in the decision-making process.

Though writing, as outlined in the national curriculum, should be approached in a systematic way if pupils are to become proficient, there is something to be said for encouraging pupils to write without worrying too much about inaccuracies. Committing one's ideas to paper implies that one is at least writing something of import rather than simply completing another exercise. It is only once writing activities are given a higher profile than recording vocabulary or answers to questions that pupils will see it as another means of communication,

> they write what they want to write and consequently writing is an enjoyable experience.
>
> (Byrne 1988: 22)

Having said this, we do well to remember, however, that pupils must read, research or be given the language to work with. They will need to be trained to simplify ideas so that they can express themselves within their own vocabulary. They need to be aware that learning a language does not happen overnight and that even those with a high degree of proficiency often find themselves simplifying language in a way they would not need to do in their mother tongue.

Redrafting is an important element of the creative writing process – a point emphasised in the national curriculum for English. The teacher may take the role of editor leading a discussion with a pupil or group of pupils about a particular piece of work. This certainly would not be possible for every piece of written work for every pupil but an occasional such conversation shows that the teacher has an interest and respect for the creative output of the individual or group. With the availability of wordprocessing and desktop publishing facilities in schools becoming commonplace, the redrafting process is much less painful than it used to be. Terry Atkinson discovered during a project on creative writing and information technology that pupils spent more time on writing when using the wordprocessor, that more interaction took place and that they were eager to read the work of others and to have their work read. He quotes the research of Schwartz, who writes that the use of the wordprocessor 'seems both psychologically and technically suited to help the writer write more and risk more and achieve more fully developed writing' (in Atkinson 1992). It is also evident that, in addition to aiding the creative process, IT stimulates a higher degree of accuracy.

CREATIVE WRITING IN PRACTICE

The Cambridgeshire foreign language poetry writing project

This project was set up in order to encourage pupils aged 11 to 18 to read some poetry in the foreign language and to write their own. The conviction was that poetry could serve as a way of enhancing the learners' feel for the language and the intention was to show how learners with even a small amount of language could manipulate what they had to express their feelings about non-trivial areas of their experience. Poetry writing was chosen because of its universality – everyone is familiar with the form to some extent – and because it allows the use of a variety of linguistic devices. As stimuli, ideas for model poems were used which teachers could present to classes for experimentation. Many of these were culled from English teaching colleagues. Though many pupils began with a model in group and class poetry writing activities, they often moved away from this to create their own very original work. Over half of the schools in the county participated in the project and submitted their pupils' work for inclusion in the county anthology entitled *A World of Words* (Cambridgeshire County Council 1990).

Some ideas for stimulating poetry writing

– This is an example of a pattern around which to work. Line 1 must answer the question Who? and so on, like this:

Line 1 Who?
Line 2 What?
Line 3 Where?
Line 4 When?
Line 5 Why?

This is an example in English:

'A Marriage of Convenience'
My friend Joan (Who?)
Married an Italian (What?)
In Rome (Where?)
Last year (When?)
She likes spaghetti (Why?)
Perhaps that's why!

A.S.

Another pattern might be the repetition of a word at the beginning of each line, for example:

'Bonjour et au revoir'
Bonjour matin
Au revoir sommeil
Bonjour devoirs
Au revoir liberté
Bonjour Noël
Au revoir argent
Bonjour été
Au revoir neige
Bonjour frère
Au revoir solitude
Bonjour nuit
Au revoir soleil
Bonjour beau garçon
Au revoir coeur

(Caroline Priestley, Longsands Community College)

– A catchy phrase is repeated at the beginning or end of each verse of the poem. Examples might be: When school's out; That's my favourite thing; Once upon a time.

– Concrete poetry
This is when the poem is written in the shape of the subject of the poem – if it's about a cat, then it will look like a picture of a cat on the page.

– Acrostic
This is where a word is written vertically on the page and a poem is created by using the letters for the first word of each line; for example:

'PAIN'
Pouvez-vous donner
A ce monsieur-là,
Insolent au comptoir,
Neuf brioches et une gifle avec ça!
A.S.

– Riddles
This is where the poet describes one thing in terms of another, leaving the reader to guess the title of the poem; for example:

E l'inferno del cielo
E il cielo dell' inferno, cos'é? La Terra
(Kassim Kurji, The John Mansfield School)

– Recipe poems
The poem takes the form of a recipe but it describes something, maybe abstract, not usually described in such concrete terms; for example:

'La Recette pour une personne sympa'
Prenez une personne,
Ajoutez un bon esprit,
Et un coeur gentil,
Et mélangez ensemble.

Prenez une tête qui réfléchit bien,
Une voix qui calme, et
Ajoutez un rayon de bonheur,
Mélangez,
Et voilà une personne SYMPA.
(William Makower, Alastair Dant,
James Gill, The Netherhall School)

Christiane Montlibert outlines ideas on preparing whole class or group poetry writing in *Letting Go, Taking Hold* (Page 1992).

Though poetry writing is often ignored as a creative tool for adolescents learning a foreign language and though it is an activity which does not appeal to all learners, the Cambridgeshire experience certainly bears out Brian Powell's statement:

> The process of writing is a bringing to the surface of feelings which, but for the creative act, might never have been expressed at all. Hence, poetry writing gives the pupil an opportunity to transform his (or her) feelings into productive force.

(Powell, 1968)

Certainly many of the poets who were published in the anthology made a strong personal investment in their work and began to see the foreign language as a means of communicating deeper thoughts than they had hitherto considered.

Working in a crowded curriculum means that the demands on pupils are probably greater than they have ever been. As language teachers, we would do well to remember that it can be a strain to demand of pupils that they listen and speak so much in the classroom. Reading and writing activities are much more under the control of the learner in terms of, for example, the rate at which the work is done and as such are important in terms of building learner independence. We must move learners on from the practice stage to what Hawkins (1981) calls the 'performance stage'. In doing this we must inject strategies for tapping pupils' creative depths and break free from the banal world of bread-buying and bus tickets. This is the only way we can expect to motivate our learners, and the only way that we shall persuade learners that communicating in a foreign language can be as effective a way of communicating as their mother tongue. The written word is an integral part of this and we must desist from presenting it as a tedious task of recording that which has been 'learnt'. Rough paper should be a well-used resource for budding linguists, for everything which is written is not sacred. The sense of achievement from creating an imaginative piece of written work in a foreign language is something which every learner should, if only once, experience sometime in his or her school career.

REFERENCES

Atkinson, T. (1992) 'Creative writing and IT', *Language Learning Journal*, September.

Byrne, D. (1988) *Teaching writing skills*, Longman.

Cambridge County Council (1990) *A World of Words: poems in foreign languages from Cambridgeshire schools*, Cambridgeshire County Council.

Department of Education and Science (1991) *Modern Foreign Languages in the National Curriculum*, HMSO.

Hawkins, E. (1981) *Modern Languages in the Curriculum*, Cambridge University Press.

Little, D., Devitt, S. and Singleton, D. (1989) *Learning Foreign Languages from Authentic Texts: theory and practice*, Authentik in association with CILT.

Page, B. (ed.) (1992) *Letting Go, Taking Hold*, Centre for Information on Language Teaching and Research (CILT).

Powell, B. (1968) *English Through Poetry Writing*, Heinemann Educational.

Rivers, W. (1968) *Teaching Foreign Language Skills*, University of Chicago Press.

Strang, R. (1959) *Creativity of Gifted and Talented Children*, Bureau of Publications, Teachers College, Columbia University.

Woods, S. (1986) 'Developing writing skills in the context of GSCE', in *Teaching Modern Languages for the GCSE*, British Association for Language Teaching and the Modern Language Association.

Wringe, C. (1989) *The Effective Teaching of Modern Languages*, Longman.

Chapter 17

Drama techniques in language teaching

Alan Maley and Alan Duff

Let us be clear from the start what we mean by 'dramatic activities'. They are activities which give the student an opportunity to use his or her own personality in creating the material on which *part* of the language class is to be based. These activities draw on the natural ability of every person to imitate, mimic and express himself or herself through gesture. They draw, too, on the student's imagination and memory, and natural capacity to bring to life parts of his or her past experience that might never otherwise emerge. They are dramatic because they arouse our interest, which they do by drawing on the unpredictable power generated when one person is brought together with others. Each student brings a different life, a different background into the class. We would like students to be able to use this when working with others.

Before going on, let us be clear what we do *not* mean by dramatic activities. We do not mean putting on plays in front of a passive audience. The stiff, self-conscious 'dramatisation' of dialogues and short sketches, as occasionally produced for distraction or language re-inforcement, is not what we have in mind here. Words, other people's words, which have been mechanically memorised, can turn to ashes in the speaker's mouth. They lose their savour even before they are spoken, and this we do not want.

Nor do we want students to feel that dramatic activities are part of the preparation for some great final performance. Their value is not in what they lead up to but in what they *are*, in what they bring out right *now*. So, in describing these ideas, we have no audience in mind other than the people who are *taking part*. Nobody looks on. This does not, however, exclude the performance by one group for another or even by one group for all the others, if the need is felt.

Lastly, as we see them, dramatic activities are not a substitute for the psychoanalyst's couch. They are not sessions of self-liberation (complexes and hang-ups cannot be cured through them). On the other hand, they will certainly release imagination and energy – and this is hard to do in language teaching. Indeed, this is one of the purely *educational* objectives that takes us well beyond the limitations of teaching the foreign language as a subject.

ABOUT LANGUAGE

Most of us are familiar with the early stages of learning at least one foreign language. We may at certain times question, uneasily, the value of what we are learning; the language may seem irrelevant or artificial, the structures unwieldy, the vocabulary far-fetched. Yet we struggle on, saying, 'Son chapeau est sur la chaise', 'The pupils are opening their books', or 'Mein Brüder hat es mir gesagt', in the belief that if the sentences are meaningful and correctly formed we must be learning something from them.

Much has changed in language teaching, but it is still true that the conviction that *Vocabulary + Essential Structures = Language* lies at the base of nearly every foreign language syllabus. Teaching on these lines takes account of only one aspect of the language – the intellectual aspect. But language is not purely an intellectual matter. Our minds are attached to our bodies, and our bodies to our minds. The intellect rarely functions without an element of emotion, yet it is so often just this element that is lacking in teaching material.

Many of the skills we most need when speaking a language, foreign or not, are those which are given *least* attention in the traditional textbook: adaptability (i.e. the ability to match one's speech to the person one is talking to), speed of reaction, sensitivity to tone, insight, anticipation; in short, *appropriateness*. The people we speak to during the day are not (thank goodness!) faceless citizens with conveniently pronounceable names like Brown and Grey, who rarely state anything but the obvious, and whose opinions are so bland as to give neither offence nor pleasure. The people we meet are busy, irritable, worried, flustered, tired, headachy; their breath smells, their armpits itch, food gets stuck between their teeth; they have quirks and tics and mannerisms, they speak too slowly or too fast, repeat themselves or lose the thread. They are not necessarily interesting but they are alive. And so are we. In order to talk to these people, we need to know who they are and who we are. We need to know whether the difference in our ages matters, whether we are likely to see them again, whether it is worth trying to influence them, whether they are likely to be helpful or difficult, etc. It is all very well to be able to produce statements like 'Had we not told them, they would not have come', but the words mean nothing unless we know who 'they' are and why this was said.

Drama attempts to put back some of this forgotten emotional content into language – and to put the body back too. This does not mean that we must suddenly start leaping about the room in an exaggerated fashion, but it does imply that we need to take more account of *meaning*. Much language teaching is done through structures or so-called situations in the belief that once a sentence has been correctly formulated a use can always be found for it. First comes form, then meaning. This approach can be misleading, even dangerous, because it accustoms the learner to making sentences fit into structural moulds. To use an analogy, such a learner is like an architect who designs a building before inspecting the site on which it is to be placed. There may be nothing structurally wrong with the design, but if the building is five storeys high with a stone façade, and is intended to fill the gap between two steel-and-glass skyscrapers, the architect will clearly have to put in some overtime! Practically any sentence will have an abstract meaning – a propositional or dictionary meaning – but this face value may have nothing to do with its concrete use.

Let us consider a few examples. The much maligned example that used to crop up on the first page of all language textbooks, 'Is this a pen?', has now disappeared (we hope). And why? Not because it was incorrect or meaning-less or useless, but because it was unnecessary and inappropriate. Try walking up to a London docker, taking a pen out of your pocket and asking him: 'Is this a pen?' If he doesn't take a swipe at you, he will most likely answer, 'What the 'ell d'you take me for?' or, 'Listen, mate, if you're looking for trouble. . . .' The question you asked was not understood as a question but as a *provocation*, which it was, for you were insulting him by suggesting he might not understand the self-evident. It is no less provoking to force the foreign language learner to go through the motions of answering inane questions simply because he or she has problems of vocabulary which the docker does not. It is not the question itself but *the reason why it was asked* that is at fault. After all, there is structurally no evident difference between 'Is this a pen?' and Macbeth's famous line, 'Is this a dagger which I see before me?' The difference lies in the feeling. Macbeth asks a question to which he knows the answer, this is true; but he asks the question because he does not want to believe what he sees. He has, then, a strong reason for speaking as he does.

Meaning, therefore, should not be confused with structure. Commands are often given in the imperative, but not always; questions are asked with question marks, but not always; continuous action in the present may be suggested by a verb ending in *-ing*, but not always. Meaning slips from one structure to another in a most elusive way. Take an innocent statement such as, 'It's eight o'clock'. This might be, variously, a substitute order ('Switch on the telly'), a concealed warning ('You'd better hurry up, they'll be here in a minute'), a form of persuasion ('Don't you think it's time we left?'), and so on. In all these examples the statement 'It's eight o'clock' takes its meaning from the intention of the speaker and his or her relation to the other person. To teach 'It's eight o'clock' as a response (and the only kind of response) to the question 'What time is it?' is to place an unnecessary restraint on the language.

Correct structures do need to be taught, nobody would deny this, but can they not be taught *meaningfully* from the very start? Consider an obvious example: the present continuous tense. This is nearly always illustrated in class by the teacher performing certain actions (opening a book, closing a window) and getting the students to reply to questions. Interest soon flags, because it seems pointless to describe what is going on in front of your eyes. Yet with a slight twist, the same actions can become interesting and the questions meaningful: all that is needed is that the observer should not know in advance why the actions are being performed. Drama, then, can help considerably by ensuring that language is used in an appropriate context, no matter how 'fantastic' this context may seem.

We realise, of course, that like all other activities in the classroom, drama activities cannot be 'real' simply because they are subject to the constraints the classroom imposes. Unlike more familiar activities, however, which always remain external to the student because imposed from without (and largely for the convenience of the teacher, not the student), these techniques draw upon precisely those internal resources which are essential for out-of-class use of the language.

ABOUT SITUATION

Is it not perhaps true that the 'context' of the drama activities is simply what the textbooks call 'situation' taking on a new guise? We think not. Situations, as presented in textbooks, tend to take account of only one aspect of context – the physical *setting*. Once this has been established, the 'characters' are lightly sketched in and left to produce their monitored 'free dialogues'. These dialogues usually take place 'At the station', 'In the restaurant' etc. Once this setting has been fixed, the cut-out figures of Mr Brown and family are put into position. Once in position, they use two kinds of language: *situational* – words such as 'ticket', 'porter', 'timetable', which are considered indispensable when one is 'At the station': *structural* – phrases which, unlike the vocabulary items, are not so much bound to the situation as enlivened by it. This is why in one book 'At the station' may serve to present the question form with WH-words ('When does the Blue Train leave?') and in another the present continuous tense ('Look, he's waving his flag!').

If one's purpose is to teach vocabulary and structure, such an approach is probably no worse than any other. But surely, then, the text-structured dialogue presentation is unnecessary? A list of words and a few correct sentences would be enough – which is exactly what most tourist phrase-books set out to provide. These books serve a specific (often useful) function: they give the rudiments of the language necessary for operating in certain surroundings. Nothing more. But most tourists have discovered to their cost that a phrase they have learnt to produce with a semblance of fluency may bring a *response* they are quite unable to follow!

How is one to right this imbalance between the great amount of material and teaching offered to students and their apparent inability to make sensible use of it? The answer is, surely, to encourage students to look at language from a different angle, to go behind the words to the actions they are most likely to perform in the language, the patterns of behaviour that lie behind all languages (*functions* such as persuading, agreeing, accepting). To do this, they need to be aware of the total situation, which is considerably richer than the mere physical setting. It will involve, at the very least, the following elements.

Setting

This is the physical environment (for example, the restaurant), which may or may not directly influence the language used, as one does not talk *only* about knives, forks, and menus at a restaurant. Physical surroundings are often incidental to what is said, for example a second-hand car may be sold in a lift, a bridge designed at a birthday party. Naturally, there are occasions when physical setting prescribes language. At the dentist's it is certain that the patient's teeth will be mentioned, but what is important is not just the hole in the tooth but the nature of the person whose tooth it is. A nervous patient will need reassuring; a mistrustful patient may need convincing; an impatient patient may have to be pacified. The dentist's role, in such cases, extends far beyond the limits of the waiting-room and the reclining chair.

Role and status

As we have seen from the last example, there is an overlap between setting and role. It is most important therefore to encourage students from the start to become sensitive to the way in which our built-in views of our own roles and those of others are defined and clarified through language. Throughout the day our roles are constantly shifting. At one moment we may find ourselves in a superior position, making decisions or giving orders; at another, we may find ourselves on the receiving end, accepting decisions and carrying out commands. To return to the dentist: at one moment he or she might say to the nurse, 'I want you to X-ray the lower left side', and a few seconds later to the patient, 'Would you mind putting your head back a little further?' These are both commands, but the choice of language depends on the dentist's relation to patient and nurse. This role would again change if the patient were, for example, a boy of eight, to whom the dentist would most likely say, 'Come on now, put your head back. That's right.'

If we deliberately ignore the roles, we end up teaching language in a vacuum. The very fact that we open our mouths to speak implies that someone will be listening. The listener is a person. Why ignore him or her?

Mood, attitude and feeling

Even in the most formal situations, people's feelings and attitudes colour their language. For obvious reasons, this often exclamatory language is difficult to teach. Yet it is necessary from the very start to express disapproval, surprise, enthusiasm, and so on. Nothing is more difficult than to work with second-hand feelings derived from texts or dialogues, yet most students are given no more than a few innocuous exclamations ('What a pity!' . . . 'How nice!' . . .) to cover all their emotional needs in the language.

Much of our feeling, especially in English, is conveyed through intonation, and it is important for students to associate the intonation pattern with the feeling that gives rise to it. Moreover, what we say will be coloured not only by our feelings but by the mood and disposition of others. Drama techniques have the singular merit of directly engaging students' feelings and, as a result, often making them aware of the need to be able to express them appropriately.

Mood and feeling also influence the grammatical form of what we say. Take, for instance, a phrase such as 'It doesn't matter'. Depending on the sincerity of the speaker, this could emerge as 'never mind', 'don't bother', 'too bad', or 'don't worry about it'.

Shared knowledge

An important element in any 'real-life' situation is shared knowledge. Run your mind over the conversations you have in the course of a typical day. Nearly all of them involve unspoken assumptions, unconscious prejudices, or shared knowledge, which may never be referred to. This is why the language of textbooks often strikes us as being artificial. The early lessons in particular abound in expressions such as 'Mr Grey's house is big', 'His car is blue', 'The blue pencil is longer than the red one'. All the above remarks are possible, but only in a restricted context: they can be taken as examples of grammatical form, and learnt as such, but because they lack internal meaning, because they are immediately demonstrable and therefore self-evident, it is difficult for students to transfer what they have learnt from them to a situation in which they might conceivably be used. This brings us back to a point made earlier – that stating the obvious is not necessarily the best way of teaching 'simple' structures. Beginner's English should make as much sense as the language of advanced students. If, therefore, both you and I know that Mr Grey's house is big, there is little point in saying so. Our shared knowledge makes the remark superfluous.

All the above elements are present in a 'situation', though any one of them may predominate. A situation is a totality, and by extracting the verbal content to study it in isolation we risk losing or deforming the meaning.

Drama can help us to restore this totality by reversing the learning process, that is, by beginning with meaning and moving to language from there.

ABOUT MOTIVATION

Much head-scratching goes on over the 'problem' of how to interest students in the language they are supposed to be learning. Many techniques have been tried – some crafty, some crude – to generate interest. Certain teachers believe that the only way is to let their students do what interests them most; often they come away disheartened: 'They aren't interested in anything', or 'They're never interested in the same thing'. Others try abandoning the textbook, but then 'The students feel they aren't learning anything'.

There can be no neat solution to motivation, but the 'problem' can be partly solved by asking, honestly, what those twenty or thirty people are trying to do *together* in the room. Surely, if communication is always on a one-to-thirty basis (i.e. from teacher to students), a great number of other possibilities are being wasted. A question from the teacher to one of the students is of direct interest to only two people in the class, though it may be of indirect interest to more. Drama helps us to keep all thirty people active all the time by making use of the dormant potential in the room. And, far from making the teacher's task harder, it actually relieves him or her of the burden of trying to do the impossible: keep thirty people active at the same intensity and at the same time. For, if the class is working in, say, five groups of six, the teacher's attention is split only in five ways and not thirty. The argument that the teacher can still not control what is happening in each group is surely spurious, for in facing the class he or she can control only one person at a time and cannot be aware of what is going on in the heads of the other twenty-nine except by constantly switching attention from one to another and keeping the students alert by cross-fire. Who then is doing *all* the work? The teacher. And what is he or she teaching?

Drama activities do not allow the teacher to gain a false sense of achievement by dispersing energy in all directions. They oblige him or her instead to stay on the edge of what is going on and not to crack the whip in the centre of the ring. They also help to get rid of the diffidence and boredom that come from being forced to stay passive most of the time. There is no place here for stereotyped responses, set-up discussions, pre-planned arguments or 'free conversations' in which everyone speaks and nobody listens, or else nobody speaks and the teacher is left to quench the fire started by his or her own burning questions. In a sense, motivation is not needed when working through drama, because the enjoyment comes from imaginative *personal* involvement, not from the sense of having successfully carried out someone else's instructions.

From the evidence to hand there is little doubt that these techniques are an extremely powerful motivational factor. Earl Stevick underlined the learner's need to feel a sense of 'belonging' (peer group acceptance) and security, and also to invest something of his own personality and so to enjoy a certain 'self esteem'. The techniques fill precisely these needs (Stevick 1976).

If drama is motivating – and we believe it is – the reason may be that it draws on the entire human resources of the class and that each technique, in its own way, yields a different, unique result every time it is practised. Nobody can predict what exactly will be thrown up in the way of ideas during these activities. This is what makes them enjoyable. Certainly we try to predict some of the language that will be needed, but the language is only part of the activity. The other part is a compound of imagination, spontaneous creation and chance discovery, which depends on the students working together.

By working together, the students learn to feel their way to creating their own parts and adapting them as they come up against others. The problem of not wanting to speak or, more often, not knowing what to say is practically resolved because the activity makes it necessary to talk. One of the more obvious explanations for this is that the students are moving *physically*, as most of us are when we talk, which means that they can change partners and break away from exchanges that might begin to flag if they were kept up too long. Another reason is that they are learning to rely on one another for their ideas and therefore using a considerable amount of language for *discussion*, argument, agreement and disagreement, organisation and execution.

It is interesting to listen to what is said at the beginning of most activities. Directive language will dominate for some time, 'You'd better . . .', 'I'll (lie on the ground) and you . . .', 'You begin, all right?' and so on. Once the skeleton of the activity has been built up, the *directive* language will be replaced by that of *discussion*, 'Wouldn't it be better if . . .?', 'I thought we were going to . . .', 'That won't work . . .'. This will be mixed in with whatever language may be involved in the sketch itself. In the final stage, we will have the language of *commentary* or *criticism*, as one of the groups tries to explain how it reacted to a sketch – 'Oh, we thought you were . . .', 'Weren't you . . .?', 'Why were you . . .?'.

This constant interchange is extremely difficult to achieve in a class where the focal point of the activity is often a text or a theme for discussion presented to a captive, seated audience. It is true that the language produced during many of the drama activities passes uncontrolled (by the teacher) and that most of what is said is heard by only two or three people, nevertheless, the whole class is actively engaged nearly all the time. Moreover, the words being 'wasted' on two or three pairs of ears are perhaps the most valuable, for every student needs periods in which to practise what he or she knows without restraint, without fear of being wrong. Students need the occasional chance to take risks in the language, to try out new ways of combination words, and of course, to find out where the gaps are in their knowledge. The drama activities give students an opportunity to strike a balance between fluency and accuracy.

FORBIDDEN TERRITORY

Language teachers sometimes behave like the owners of large estates, putting up high walls round their territory and signs saying 'No Trespassing'. In secondary schools the foreign language becomes a subject on a timetable, and it is taught as a subject rather than as a language. As a result, the teacher of English shows little interest in what his or her colleagues might be doing in German or French; he or she may be on nodding terms with the teachers of Mathematics and History, and never have met the person in charge of Music or Science.

Drama is like the naughty child who climbs the high walls and ignores the 'No Trespassing' sign. It does not allow us to define our territory so exclusively: it forces us to take as our starting-point *life* not language. And life means all subjects, whether they are on the timetable or not. Drama may involve music, history, painting, mathematics, skiing, photography, cooking – anything. It does not respect subject barriers.

The language teacher will be wise to take advantage of this to enliven his or her work. Once students have discovered that there is another world, much closer and more real than that of Mr Brown, Herr Schmidt, and M. Dupont, with their waxwork wives and children, the problem of 'how to keep their interest' will gradually disappear. And, strangest of all, this other world does not need to be conjured up with expensive equipment – all that is needed is a roomful of human beings.

REFERENCE

Stevick, E. (1976) *Memory, Meaning and Method*, Newbury House.

Chapter 18

Approche communicative
Un second souffle?

Jean-Marc Caré

L'histoire de la didactique des langues nous apprend que l'expression dramatique a souvent été liée à l'apprentissage linguistique. Les méthodes directes, puis les méthodes structurales, ont intégré dans leur démarche des phases dites de dramatisation. Elles n'ont pas toujours su le faire avec efficacité, une des raisons pour lesquelles cette phase est progressivement tombée en désuétude.

Avec la substitution progressive dans les manuels, puis dans les pratiques de classe, de l'approche structuraliste par l'approche communicative, s'est fait sentir le besoin d'une meilleure intégration du réel aux contenus de l'enseignement. L'authentique a tenté de supplanter le didactique. Mais le réel passe mal dans les classes. Les portes sont probablement trop étroites, les murs trop épais. Les approches précédentes ont toutes tenté de faire passer, sans grand succès, une réalité qui, trop encombrante, résistait. Plutôt que de s'épuiser à faire passer à toute force ce réel insaisissable, ne fallait-il pas, empruntant cette technique à la recherche scientifique, essayer de le simuler?

Cette alternative est apparue dès le début des années 1970. Dans un article du *Français dans le monde*, Francis Debyser suggérait déjà le recours aux techniques de simulation.[1] Quelques années plus tard, Alan Maley du British Council allait plus loin encore en évoquant, dans une formule percutante, l'illusion de la réalité et la réalité de l'illusion. L'introduction de techniques de simulation dans l'enseignement/apprentissage des langues étrangères n'est donc pas vraiment une nouveauté.

Ce qui me semble plus neuf, par contre, serait:

- la recherche d'une plus grande diversité et d'une meilleure complémentarité dans la mise au point de ces techniques;
- la possibilité aujourd'hui, en formation initiale ou continue, de donner plus de professionalisme aux utilisateurs potentiels que sont les professeurs et les élèves. Simuler entraîne à jouer, à représenter et donc à connaître et respecter les conventions théâtrales de base;
- le concept de simulation globale qui représente un projet de création collective plus ambitieux et plus complet.

Que sommes-nous donc amenés à proposer aujourd'hui? Nous allons tenter d'imiter le réel; nous allons essayer de faire «comme si» les choses étaient réelles, de simuler, mettant en place dans la classe les conditions d'un certain réalisme. Pour simuler, nous disposons actuellement de techniques que l'on pourrait placer comme dans le tableau 18.1 sur un axe censé représenter la spontanéité: à gauche, les techniques de dramatisation, au milieu les simulations et à droite l'improvisation.

DRAMATISATION	SIMULATION	IMPROVISATION
T E X T E	*canevas fermés*	C A N E V A S
	RUPTURE	
	canevas ouverts	
	simulation globale	

Tableau 18.1 La spontanéité dans les techniques de simulation

Quelles sont ces techniques? Comment fonctionnent-elles? A quoi servent-elles? Quand peut-on les utiliser dans l'apprentissage d'une langue étrangère?

DRAMATISATION: LA CONTRAINTE ET LE PLAISIR DU TEXTE

Nous appellerons dramatisation tout travail consistant à rendre un texte intelligible et intelligent par d'autres ressources que le linguistique: le corps, la voix, l'espace. Ici, nous aurons toujours un texte: frontière très nette entre dramatisation et simulation.

Vouloir monter une simulation en laissant aux élèves la possibilité d'écrire leurs répliques, ce n'est pas franchir cette frontière et donc rester en dramatisation.

Ce texte peut être un dialogue de méthode. Dans les méthodes SGAV (structuro-globale audio-visuel), les auteurs proposaient le recours à des techniques de dramatisation et le dialogue était appris par coeur, puis joué. Je crois qu'il est bon, dans une perspective communicative, de ne pas oublier ce genre de technique. Elle permet à l'élève, libéré de la nécessité d'avoir à construire ses phrases, de pratiquer des activités non verbales. Elle permet aussi de mémoriser des textes, et les apprendre par coeur, quand ils sont de qualité, n'est pas scandaleux, comme on l'a cru à un certain moment.

J'ai dit dialogue de méthodes, je dirai de plus en plus textes littéraires aussi. Les méthodes SGAV ont condamné un peu trop vite tout ce qui était littéraire. Avec la littérature, nous avons pourtant une véritable banque de bons dialogues à notre disposition (autant dans le théâtre que dans le roman).

Introduire progressivement ces textes, c'est permettre aux élèves de mémoriser, de jouer un écrivain et d'accéder ainsi au patrimoine culturel. Ceci peut être un peu plus gratifiant que la mémorisation de dialogues fabriqués.

SIMULATION: L'ART DE L'OUVERTURE PROGRESSIVE

Dès que l'on aborde la simulation, on quitte le texte. Cela ne veut pas dire que nous sommes soudain en face du vide. Nous allons avoir deux possibilités:

- imiter, simuler, jouer des séquences de communication *entièrement prévisibles*, parce que très stéréotypées et même fortement ritualisées. Ces situations, nous allons pouvoir les décrire d'un bout à l'autre. Par exemple, dans les relations marchandes, nous nous comportons toujours à peu près de la même manière: quand on se présente à un guichet d'embarquement dans un aéroport, il se dit toujours la même chose et il se passe toujours la même chose. Nous pouvons donc décrire en termes d'intentions communicatives ou encore d'actes de paroles, un modèle, un canevas, une matrice qui va permettre à l'élève de simuler le réel.

  Ces canevas aboutissement à des simulations entièrement programmées, donc relativement contraignantes.
- mais nous allons pouvoir aussi imiter, simuler des situations de communication plus *ouvertes parce que plus imprévisibles*. Ce sera le cas, par exemple, à mon guichet d'embarquement si une quelconque difficulté survient, une erreur dans les dates de réservation, une surcharge de bagages . . . Je ne peux plus proposer un seul canevas. Je ne peux donc plus décrire la totalité des séquences en terme d'actes de parole.

Pour revenir un peu à cette notion de canevas, je citerai le poète Jean Tardieu qui, dans une courte pièce de théâtre intitulée *Finissez vos phrases*, illustre bien ce terme. Cette pièce met en scène la rencontre de deux personnages: Monsieur A et Madame B. Monsieur A dit à Madame B: «Chère madame, quel plaisir de.» Madame B lui répond: «Oui effectivement depuis que.» Et toute la pièce est construite pour ça. C'est-à-dire qu'au fond, on a là des intentions communicatives, mais les phrases ne sont jamais entièrement réalisées.

Mon canevas va donc décrire la totalité de la situation, chaque séquence correspondant à un acte de parole.

Tranches de vie en rupture

Mais, dans la communication quotidienne, tout ne se passe pas toujours très bien. Tout n'est pas toujours prévisible et rituel. Il y a des situations dans lesquelles nous sommes en face d'un déséquilibre, d'une rupture, d'un dysfonctionnement. On ne peut plus prévoir ce qui va arriver, donc ce qui va se dire. On peut évoquer deux types de ruptures: – des ruptures physiques . . . Je prends le cas de l'ascenseur car il est typique. Quand il fonctionne bien, c'est le monde du silence. Les gens évitent de se parler, le plus souvent, se tournent le dos. S'il tombe en panne, les gens qui s'y trouvent vont tenter d'utiliser le langage pour débloquer cette situation physiquement bloquée. La notion de rupture me paraît donc importante. Elle permet de passer de modèles entièrement descriptibles et contraignants à des modèles plus ouverts.

Je disais qu'il y avait deux types de ruptures, la deuxième est psychologique parce que conflictuelle. Deux personnes désirent toutes les deux la même chose. Imaginez un seul récepteur de TV, une personne veut voir la première chaîne et l'autre la troisième. Elles se trouvent dans une situation conflictuelle. Il y a rupture et elles vont tenter de communiquer pour résoudre cette situation de conflit. Elles y arriveront ou non. On ne peut plus préjuger, à ce moment-là, du déroulement de la situation.

Donc, nous allons avoir deux types de situation de communication et deux techniques un peu différentes: la première propose un modèle complet et fermé sur lui-même. Appelons-la «*simulation contrainte, ou fermée*».

Ici, tout est prévisible. On peut décrire des intentions communicatives, mais aussi en même temps fournir les informations linguistiques correspondantes. Ceci a des conséquences pédagogiques immédiates: si nous pouvons programmer les apports linguistiques, nous sommes en mesure de suivre une progression. Nous avons donc là une technique d'apprentissage et d'acquisition linguistique.

Dans l'autre cas, nous ne pouvons décrire que le début d'une situation de communication dans laquelle nous allons injecter des ruptures potentielles. Mais nous ne pouvons plus décrire la totalité du déroulement, sinon nous nous retrouverions en simulation contrainte. Convenons d'appeler ce deuxième type de situation: «*simulation ouverte*». Nous ne sommes pas loin du jeu de rôle.

Ici, nous ne pouvons pas décider à la place des élèves d'une évolution type de la situation de départ. Nous ne pouvons plus programmer le matériel linguistique. Cette technique n'étant plus compatible avec une progression ne peut être utilisée comme technique d'apprentissage ou d'acquisition. Nous en ferons plutôt une technique d'entraînement ou encore d'évaluation de la compétence communicative, car nous avons là un bon moyen de vérifier, par étapes ou paliers, dans l'apprentissage, que nos élèves sont capables ou non de réutiliser tous leurs acquis antérieurs dans des situations où la mémorisation, le conditionnement ne suffisent plus.

Univers fictifs

Au B.E.L.C. (Bureau pour l'enseignement de la langue et de la civilisation française), nous sommes allés un peu plus loin avec ce que nous avons appelé les *simulations globales*. Le projet est d'emblée plus ambitieux puisqu'il consiste à engager les élèves dans l'invention ou la réinvention d'une partie du monde. Par exemple: inventer un immeuble parisien, en décrire l'aspect extérieur, en construire l'aménagement intérieur avec la détermination du nombre d'étages, la répartition des appartements. Puis, ayant tracé des plans, meubler progressivement les lieux. Quand le décor est planté, habiter les lieux en inventant des identités fictives d'habitants. Cette construction collective peut déboucher sur un roman, à la manière de *La vie mode d'emploi* de Georges Perec. Dans ce cas, les élèves tireront les ficelles de leurs propres personnages et feront le récit d'événements ou d'incidents du quotidien. Ils pourront ainsi, se mettant dans la peau de leurs personnages, s'engager dans un vaste jeu de rôles.

Iles est un monde suffisamment délimité, clos, pour fournir un bon support à une construction collective de ce type. Dans le cas de *l'immeuble*, nous engageons les élèves dans la reconstruction d'un monde plausible en les faisant se rapprocher le plus possible de l'univers d'un immeuble parisien. Mais nous pourrions tout aussi bien opter pour une autre réalité. Nous tentons en tout cas de ne pas trop trahir le réel. L'imaginaire est ici au coin de la rue.

Avec *Iles*, nous essayons d'échapper momentanément au réel en permettant aux élèves de refaire le monde à leur manière, d'imaginer un univers neuf si possible, sans rapport avec le monde connu. En inventant une faune, une flore nouvelles, ils construisent progressivement une île imaginaire sur laquelle ils vont, après avoir fait naufrage, s'installer et vivre, le temps de la simulation.

Nous proposons aussi de travailler sur *le cirque*, autre monde clos et facilement délimitable. Nous sommes ici entre un réel et un imaginaire qui conviennent assez bien à un public d'enfants ou de très jeunes adolescents.

Nous travaillons en ce moment à la mise au point d'une quatrième simulation globale: *le Village* qui sera probablement la plus pédagogique de toutes, parce que plus ouverte sur la globalité du monde, entre l'urbain et le rural et, probablement utilisable très tôt dans l'apprentissage, avec des débutants.

Ces simulations globales sont évidemment plus ambitieuses que les simulations contraintes et les jeux de rôles. Elles demandent un investissement temporel plus important: une quinzaine d'heures pour planter un décor plausible, auquel les élèves puissent s'attacher; une cinquantaine d'heures pour le faire évoluer dans le temps, le faire vivre, pour passer de la description au récit.

IMPROVISATION: UNE AUTRE DIMENSION

Sur l'axe de départ, censé représenter la spontanéité, j'ai posé une première frontière, celle du texte, puis une seconde, celle du canevas. Au-delà, c'est en face du vide ou presque, devant l'inconnu, l'imprévu. Et il faut tenter de passer cette dernière frontière, qu'il faut pousser les élèves à aller encore plus loin. Parce qu'il y a de vieilles croyances qui traînent encore dans la tête des professeurs: cette idée qu'il faut absolument passer par un probatoire fait d'acquisitions linguistiques conditionnées et répétitives, en gros une centaine d'heures de dressage, avant de pouvoir enfin prendre des risques, avoir le droit à l'expression spontanée, personnelle, à une communication moins didactique. Cette idée imprègne encore bien des pratiques de classe; elle est un obstacle de taille au développement de l'approche communicative. Ce long probatoire nuit à la spontanéité. La liberté surveillée, bureaucratique à force d'être assise, devient vite une habitude. L'élève s'installe progressivement dans ce confort initial. Pourquoi alors, plus tard, avoir à prendre l'initiative du risque?

Or, au-delà de cette dernière frontière, c'est l'improvisation. Le canevas dépassé, on est en face du vide. On doit non seulement faire ses phrases mais aussi décider de tout le reste: je construis mon personnage, je décide de prendre ou d'abandonner la parole et surtout, je suis le seul à décider de ce que je vais dire.

De quoi va-t-on se servir pour stimuler cette capacité d'improvisation? Ce ne sera plus un texte ou des intentions communicatives. Ce sera par exemple un geste, un simple geste qui va pouvoir déclencher une conversation. Donc, plus de support textuel ou discursif mais ce que certains didacticiens ont appelé des déclencheurs: ces petits mots de la conversation que sont les: «pardon, excusez-moi, s'il vous plaît, vous savez, écoutez, dites, excusez-moi de vous déranger, etc.», sont aussi autant de déclencheurs potentiels.

Plus tard, à la manière des ligues d'improvisation, nous pourrons partir de thèmes. Imaginons des débutants au bout d'une quinzaine d'heures, ayant appris les rudiments des salutations de l'identification personnelle en français. On pourra leur proposer d'improviser des rencontres déjà inhabituelles:

– avec un sourd, avec un cheval ou un lion, avec soi-même ou son double, etc.

C'est-à-dire essayer de leur faire réutiliser le plus de moyens linguistiques acquis en faisant jouer toutes les ressources non verbales et en faisant appel à leur imagination et à leur fantaisie.

Avec ces techniques, nous nous rapprocherons de la spontanéité que nos élèves connaissent en langue maternelle, même si au début les productions verbales paraîtront encore maladroites et limitées. L'essentiel, c'est que ne soit pas retardée cette expérience de l'imprévu.

UNE OUVERTURE MÉTHODOLOGIQUE

Cet inventaire laisse entrevoir une progression quasi naturelle. On commencera bien sûr plutôt par des dramatisations puisque l'élève, libéré de la nécessité d'avoir à faire des phrases, pourra concentrer toute son attention sur tout le travail théâtral: articulation correcte, rythme et intonation, gestuelle.

Par la suite, on l'engagera progressivement à tenter de simuler des situations de communication contraintes, à partir de canevas entièrement programmables. Puis, quittant ces belles machines où tout fonctionne presque trop bien, on proposera des ruptures pour aller vers plus d'imprévu. Enfin, par le biais de déclencheurs verbaux et non verbaux, et en se privant de tout support linguistique, on ira jusqu'à l'improvisation. Nous disposons là d'un ensemble d'outils qui, mis en oeuvre selon une progression raisonnée et raisonnable, devraient très certainement contribuer à orienter l'approche communicative des années 1990 vers une conception plus pragmatique (au sens linguistique du terme) de l'apprentissage linguistique. Un meilleur dosage des activités formelles de manipulation grammaticale et des activités sémantiques de production (orale ou écrite), un meilleur rapport entre fonctionnel, réel, utile et imaginaire et poétique, plus de professionnalisme chez les enseignants dans la maîtrise de leurs outils seront autant d'occasions de maintenir un français dynamique, une langue équilibrée.

Il n'y a pas vraiment de mauvaises méthodes comme il n'y a pas vraiment de mauvaises recettes. Mais, en se trompant d'ingrédients ou de dosage, on peut faire de la mauvaise cuisine. Et la didactique, quand elle consent à descendre dans la classe, est, comme la cuisine, affaire de dosage.

Ces rééquilibrages réussis, on devrait pouvoir, même modestement dans les pratiques quotidiennes de classe, rapprocher langue et langages, forme et sens, grammaire et communication, couples ailleurs solidaires depuis toujours.

Il faut espérer qu'alors l'approche communicative, menacée aujourd'hui de n'être bientôt plus qu'un coeur pieux, un espoir déçu, une étiquette de plus, pourra connaître son second souffle.

NOTE

1 Debyser, F. (1974) «*Simulation et réalité dans l'enseignement des langues vivantes. Le français dans le monde, n° 104 et 106*».

Chapter 19

Role activities in the foreign language classroom

Barrie K. Joy

INTRODUCTION

This chapter attempts to set role activities in foreign language education within a sociolinguistic and psychological frame of reference which seeks to take account of

- the complex behaviours involved in interacting and negotiating with meaning and purpose in a foreign culture;
- the kinds of learning contexts these behaviours imply; and
- the types of knowledge, skills and strategies which it is necessary for individual learners to develop if they are to apprise and realise verbal and non-verbal meanings in culturally appropriate ways.

LEARNING SOCIAL ROLES IN CONTEXT

A social role may be briefly defined as the set of appropriate behaviours expected from a particular person or status in relation to a particular situation or context. These behaviours are transacted largely in patterned interaction with others on a basis of culturally shared meanings and perceptions.

Native speakers learn from an early age not just what to say but also when to say it, to whom, in certain ways in a range of circumstances, for example, face-to-face, on the telephone and in letters. From a sociolinguistic perspective, how to communicate with an inventory of registers – the forms of language associated with a particular social situation or subject matter – is learned as an integral part of the cultures, norms and mores of our society. In the process of becoming socialised we learn and practise, often to the point of unconscious habit, not only what to say or write in certain situations, but what to say we listen to, watch or read, when to say nothing, when to speak in certain ways, when to smile, how to address a range of people in a range of ways, when to stand up, sit down, how and when to arrive and leave. In short, to behave 'in role' is to behave acceptably in culturally defined ways.

And even the eccentric or rebel needs to be familiar with 'taking roles' before 'making' or 'breaking' them.

Within social psychology, 'script theory' is based on the idea that social life can be analysed into behavioural frames of reference, for each of which there is a superordinate script, for example 'going to a restaurant', and a number of sub-scripts for constituent variants, such as *restaurant de cinq étoiles*, *relais routier*, café, snack-bar, *Imbißstube*, McDonalds, Chinese take-away, roadside canteen. Each sub-script has an associated set of sequences and patterns of behaviour. All catering establishments share the assumption that you will order, receive and pay for food and/or drink. But what you would expect to order, the level of service, the time it takes, what you would pay and the forms of behaviour and communication you would expect to encounter and to use would vary significantly.

To explain in relation to script theory how we cope when faced with a new context, Athay and Darley have developed the concept of 'interaction competencies'.

> We use this term to designate capacities to construct innovative patterns of performance by reconstructing familiar, practised paradigms to meet the particular demands of varying interaction situations. The competencies are skills in the construction of cognitive schemes and performance patterns in such a fashion as to cope with situational specificities while at the same time preserving sufficient continuity with established routines to sustain the sense of command that comes only with application of familiar, matter-of-course procedures.
>
> (Athay and Darley 1981)

Within a culture or sub-culture certain behaviours would be less or more familiar even to groups of native speakers or individuals. British institutions called 'finishing schools' provide access for an élite to an explicit repertoire of roles and behaviours, including language, which are unfamiliar to most British people and have to be taught, learned and practised to acceptable levels of competence.

Most learners of a foreign language have to learn *ab initio* the appropriate norms, roles and communicative behaviours of the target culture. Significantly, because of time constraints and the tradition of foreign language teaching in this country, emphases tend to be placed quickly on forms of language and language formulae rather than on the presentation of language in its proper cultural contexts. The resulting 'role activities' can become somewhat superficial – illustrating how actual practice and outcomes can fall disappointingly short of the rich potential which true-to-life foreign language studies should offer learners in our schools and colleges.

ROLE ACTIVITIES IN FOREIGN LANGUAGE EDUCATION

There is considerable variation, even confusion, in the understanding of the term 'role' in foreign language education. Some teachers are very enthusiastic and skilled in its application; others have tried and abandoned it; many feel uncomfortable in its use. Role activities are variously understood as ranging from fairly stylised, simplistic, short, formulaic and somewhat predictable routine interchanges, through creative variations on a theme, to extended open-ended, complex and demanding simulations and improvisations. Gumperz distinguishes usefully between transacted (buying a ticket at the station) and personalised (socialising with friends) interaction. What is required, however, is an approach to role activities which systematically develops these two and other categories of interaction. Ideally, this would take into account the studies of 'interlanguages' in terms of the expectations of a foreigner as to how an English person is likely to interact, as well as how the English person interprets the expectations of the foreigner in respect of his behaviour. Presently, most role activities in most classrooms are conceived as oral interactions involving normally two or more actors. It is clear, however, that writing in French, be it a postcard to a friend or a letter to a newspaper, also conforms to certain 'rule-like' conventions and expectations. In short, one is behaving 'in role' in accordance with certain cultural expectations which tend to guide, though not dictate, minute details of social life.

The danger is that, unless we can bring learners systematically to observe the patterns of the culture as well as its language, they will tend to assume that, with a few quirky exceptions, things are done similarly in the target culture as in their own and that it is only the language, not the culture, which is different in form and structure. Genuine role studies and activities in the foreign language help develop a comparative perspective by objectifying, exploding and problematising situations and contexts of the target culture and the behaviours of its users, including language as a central feature, to show that it cannot be taken for granted that the learner's cultural assumptions and interactions are identical with those of the native speaker. Some behaviours may be universalistic and others highly particularistic with regard to the two cultures. As Zurcher states:

> In seeking to combine the two traditionally polarised sociological rôle models of the social order as societally determined puppet and as creative free agent any analysis of rôle enactment must first examine the underlying local assumptions about the nature of human beings and society, and then the situation-specific individual behavioural expectations.
>
> (Zurcher 1983)

Role activities offer rich opportunities to transcend the mere routinised practice and repetition of foreign language forms to enable learners to behave with them appropriately and discerningly in a range of contexts. As such, they should be included from the very earliest lessons, not repeatedly deferred until learners have 'more' language. Rather it is a question of what they do with the language they have and how the language of the programme is informed by the uses to which it is to be put. Importantly, learners improve their abilities to interact by actually interacting – not by only preparing to do so. In consequence, we may need to increase our resolve to ensure that the genuine complexity of learning to observe and communicate in a foreign language, involving the meanings behind the words and signs, in a hermeneutic and semiotic sense of negotiated and interpreted systems of meaning, figures more centrally in our programmes of studies.

THE FOREIGN LANGUAGE CLASSROOM AS COMMUNICATIVE LANGUAGE LABORATORY

Culturally informed role activities can be employed flexibly in most approaches to foreign language learning but are particularly appropriate to communicative language programmes where emphasis is laid upon behaving with appropriate language derived from a descriptive linguistic analysis rather than upon analysing language in accordance with a prescriptive grammatical model. Communicating orally in a foreign language does, of course, normally involve meaningful verbal language as a key component, but also involved are a whole range of other features, such as gestures, miens, proxemics, silences and hesitation phenomena, all of which complement or convey special contextualised meanings.

Actual role behaviour is rarely neutral or reducible to a script in an absolute sense. Even basic formulaic interchanges are often personalised by particular intonations, a pause, a frown, a smile. Role activities, properly understood, require knowledge about the target culture and language to be regularly converted into discerning and informed communicative behaviours. As such, they involve fundamentally what I will call 'the fifth language skill' – observing how people behave in communicating in the target culture and comparing this with one's own communicative behaviour.

Role activities in the active classroom can offer a bridge to authentic cultural interaction and natural language use. Certainly, they can simulate aspects of set situations appropriate to, say, the tourist wishing to negotiate aspects of the target culture. As such they provide instant gratification – a product, a result! Equally, they can provide contextualised practice in the kind of interactions and language which exchange pupils are likely to encounter in their host family – the reception, introductions to the family, coping with the different aspects of the extended French dinner. They enable learners to initiate as well as respond to language, and the individual learner to rehearse aspects of language use generated by personally identified communicative needs on the basis of projected social interactions.

Such activities might usefully include exposing learners to natural language of a more complex and demanding level to familiarise the learner with the role of interacting on the basis of gist comprehension. Opportunity should also be provided for learners 'in role' to practise forms of language which enable them to ask for clarification of particular words and information in interaction with a native speaker who is largely unaware of the need to adjust language use to the speaker. Clearly, the use in the classroom of a truly sympathetic language assistant or native speaker as a role partner could be most beneficial for such specific purposes.

Authentic role activities in the foreign language are most effectively studied in classrooms which are in the original sense 'language laboratories', where learners are encouraged to observe, analyse, reflect on, experiment with, and practise communicating and behaving in the target culture in focused, disciplined and systematic ways. The study of roles in interactive language classrooms provides learners with the opportunity to experience language behaviour, to refine their understanding of the relationship between language and context, to learn to mean more precisely and more effectively, and to extend their abilities to interact. Learners should come to understand that language is not only context-sensitive but that language can change the context. This dynamic nature of language is well reflected in genuinely interactive role activities. The 'language laboratory' should provide a secure environment in which learners develop the ability to interpret the target culture by comparing it with their own and to see the strange as familiar and the familiar as strange and the need to communicate differently. They can learn to risk-take, and to dare to extend their own communicative power through language interactions in which they are personally engaged.

As an example of role behaviour in foreign language studies let us take the idea of s'embrasser in French. Native French speakers will know immediately whether it is appropriate or not in a given context, or whether a handshake would be more appropriate. They read the situation and behave appropriately in accordance with the perceived 'script'. A foreigner needs to learn to identify the critical features of this situation – particularly how the options available are determined by the relationship between the social actors. Armed with such awareness, what observable behaviour actually occurs?

Close analysis would show distinctive differences between the 'haptics' of the English and French handshakes – their purpose, frequency and manner. In relation to 's'embrasser' the non-native speaker would need to know that it involves two 'passes' between people living outside, and four between people living inside, the Paris area; it can involve actual kissing on each cheek if the relationship is a familial one or one of close friendship, especially if two females are involved. In less familiar relationships that are perceived as closer than those requiring a handshake, the cheeks are lightly touched and a kissing noise is made – without an actual kiss taking place! The reciprocal positioning of arms placed lightly on the shoulders or behind the back has been practised to the point of non-confusion by generations of French natives. But for an English pupil the contexts of occurrence as well as the actions themselves will require informed and well-aimed practice!

We have not yet mentioned the verbal language forms and possible non-verbal gestures which might accompany the various appropriate actions – and these will present a further variety of choices of form and interaction patterns. There are, of course, occasions when none of these possible combinations would be used by French native speakers. What is often of interest to British secondary school pupils is that most of their French contemporaries *s'embrassent* irrespective of the sex of their peers. If time is taken to ensure that learners understand the choices involved and the behaviours implied, and to specify carefully the practice contexts so that learners are psychologically 'in role' and their decisions are 'real', they find greetings an interesting and enjoyable aspect of French culture, and frequently begin to compare them with British forms of greeting. However, if dealt with superficially, the game can be quickly lost. Roles, or more accurately non-roles, become trivial and perfunctory, demotivate and leave stereotypes about the 'funny French' unchallenged.

Native speakers can project, rehearse and prepare mentally the language and strategies which are likely to be appropriate to a particular interaction. Non-native learners can do this only if they understand the 'rules' of discourse in the culture – for example, turn-taking, acceptable/unacceptable manners of making or challenging a statement and the corresponding moves and strategies as well as the language forms necessary to participate effectively in the game-like activity of communicating with others. As Barnes and Rosen observe:

> Language activities have definite functions to perform and can be likened to games because they have 'rules' for all 'players' and only certain moves are possible. Players have to learn the language rules and how various parts of the game are related.
>
> (Barnes *et al.* 1969)

Cue cards can help in preparing learners for structured role interactions. Learner A knows he has to greet learner B and vice versa. In the earliest lessons the language elements will need to be given, but as the course progresses both A and B may choose from a repertoire of greetings once they know the context. Cue cards can help provide a framework of interaction to learners at different levels and may vary in their form, content and complexity according to the ability of learners to take or make roles.

It is essential to inculcate in students from the very beginning the need for close attention to detail with regard to pronunciation and expression.

Learners should be encouraged to use a tape-recorder at home for focused listening to spoken language so that the elements are well rehearsed before the role enactments. It is critically important that even the first interchanges – e.g. *Bonjour, Michelle! Bonjour, Jean! Ça va? Oui, ça va. Et toi? Oui, ça va bien* – are practised with proper engagement and expression by learners. Variants should not be practised automatically just for the sake of it, but because the specified context and roles make a particular variant more appropriate.

The language surrounding role can also be a fruitful source of, and springboard to, learning. Learners might read about forms of greeting in French, view a video illustrating forms of greeting or write to penfriends to obtain further information. Role activities can be based on, or stimulate use of, a variety of materials, including newspaper, radio and television sources. The oral and/or written nature of the materials allows role activities to be linked with, and further develop, the four macro-skills of language in both discrete and combined forms. The writing of scripts set within written narrative, informed by careful listening to tapes of situations would be an example of such work. In informing the group about key aspects of the interaction, the teacher would contextualise as far as possible in French, and model roles in French to immerse learners in the contexts to give them a 'feel' for the range of possible interactions, which they would then perform in a variety of carefully defined contexts and role relationships.

Students also need opportunities to analyse the roles of the characters involved in terms of personality, in order to give force to their interactions and motive for their personal interpretations of behaviour, and to discuss the language and the strategies they intend to use. Let us take an example with, say, a group of 15-year-old Year 10 pupils learning French.

SETTING UP A ROLE ACTIVITY

Au restaurant

Essentially there are three stages in setting up a role activity: briefing, interaction and debriefing.

Briefing

This involves setting the scene, giving instructions, modelling, preparing and providing guidance, and allocating roles. As far as possible this should be done in the foreign language. For learners to succeed they must be well briefed, clear as to what is expected of them and well prepared in the basic language and paralinguistic features required by the particular roles. These must be pitched at an appropriate level of demand: if they are too difficult, learners will feel thwarted and quickly lose enthusiasm, because the requirement to perform effectively 'in role' will be constantly cut across by inadequate coverage of the constituent elements. In particular, learners should not enter a role enactment with a script in their hand from which they read aloud, as this does not allow them to focus on, and respond to, the interaction. If the preparation has been thorough, role activities will still be demanding because they involve a spontaneous bringing together of knowledge and skills in behaviour. Learners must be linguistically and psychologically *prepared* to take on the challenge.

It is often helpful to students to have a 'warm-up' session. Stanislavski used to require of his students that they practise expressing 'tonight' in fifty different ways – with joy, fear, anger, invitationally, threateningly, etc. Warm-ups can also be conducted without learners using the language themselves, but rather acting, reacting and interacting with each other in mime in response to the instructions or suggestions of the teacher in the foreign language: '*Vous êtes un client au restaurant. Lisez le menu. Vous êtes un garçon. Apportez le plat aux clients à la table*', etc.

The teacher (or, in more advanced classes, perhaps the learner) sets the scene.

> '*Nous sommes au restaurant. Voici les tables, les garçons, le menu, etc. Vous désirez le menu. Qu'est-ce que vous dites? Il ne vous remarque pas. Qu'est-ce que vous faites pour attirer son attention? Garçon, s'il vous plaît! Il vient et vous apporte le menu. Il est très beau, attentionné. Décrivez-le – les vêtements, son air, son tempérament!*' [At this point the teacher might introduce a picture or photograph of the individual or a reference in order to reinforce the distinctive character and role of this particular waiter.] '*Il s'occupe bien de vous. Il vous explique le menu et vous donnez votre commande. Qu'est-ce que vous voulez? Oui, un grand steak, des pommes frites et des légumes mixtes. Après quelques minutes il apporte le plat et dit, "Bon appétit!" Vous avez mangé le plat et le garçon reprend sa tâche. "C'était bon?" "Un dessert, monsieur?" Vous êtes pressé. "Merci, je dois partir. L'addition, s'il vous plaît."* '

Contrast this scene with another.

> '*Ce garçon est impoli et brusque. Vous donnez votre commande – vous voulez commander un steak en sauce avec des légumes et des frites mais vous voulez poser des questions sur la sauce. Il est impatient, sans soin. Vous êtes mal à l'aise. Vous voulez lui donner un pourboire? Pourquoi pas? Vous avez une allergie à l'ail. Ses réponses sont vagues – il ne répond pas vraiment à vos questions. "C'est une sauce normale, monsieur." Il apporte le steak. Ça pue l'ail! Vous êtes allergique à l'ail. Vous expliquez votre problème mais il n'y prête pas attention. Il dit "Bof. C'est normal, monsieur. Vous êtes en France. Ici on le fait comme ça!" Vous protestez. "Mais, je ne peux pas le manger. Je veux voir le patron, s'il vous plaît." Il*

répond "Bon, d'accord, monsieur! Mais cela ne changera rien!" Le patron vient. Sa manière est aggressive. Vous vous fâchez contre lui. "Sans doute c'est de sa faute!" "Mais non, monsieur! Vous n'avez pas precisé votre allergie à l'ail", etc.'

Having talked through the roles and the interactions, it is important to reinforce certain critical features, e.g. *Ça pue l'ail! – C'est de votre faute.* The learners should then have further opportunity to clarify their own thinking, to ask questions, to add and check ideas of their own. Can they outline in French what is going to take place? Encourage them to discuss movements, expressions, intonation, possible language variants, etc. in plenary small groups and pairs.

Learners often choose the more awkward situation or character, and it is important that they do not exaggerate and over-step the bounds of credibility! But such interactions do occur, and the learners must do all they can with their available communicative resources to cope. At this level the teacher can extend their learning of contextualised comprehension by pitching the language at times a little above their active repertoire. Cumulatively, this helps prepare learners for the cut-and-thrust of unedited natural language which they will encounter in a French-speaking culture.

Roles are then allocated including particular foci for 'observers'.

Interaction

Depending on the abilities of the learners, interactions can now proceed – either with one pair first modelling their enactment for the whole group or directly in pairs. It is often helpful if the teacher has a particular sign, for example snapping the fingers, to switch learners crisply 'into role'.

As far as possible learners should be left to their own resources but the teacher should be readily available to assist, if required. The teacher has many functions in role activities and these require considerable flexibility. In effect, the role-oriented classroom becomes a briefing, rehearsal and performance studio, and the teacher alternates between the roles of stage manager, director, producer, narrator–commentator, model, partner, animateur, prompter, monitor and evaluator. A key task is to enable and facilitate, to support learners where necessary but not prematurely. Above all, any inclination to interrupt the actual 'in role' performance of learners must be controlled, as this breaks precisely the psychological context which the teacher has worked hard to create. Once the interaction has taken place, an agreed signal, for example a loud hand-clap, helps to re-focus quickly the attention of all learners in preparation for the debriefing. This should take place while the activity is still fresh in minds.

Debriefing

The debriefing should focus first on successful aspects of the performance. Comments should then be invited on any problems encountered, or observed by other learners, in terms of the language or the behaviours. The use of the tape-recorder and video-recorder are of great value at this review stage and provide the basis for detailed analysis and discussion – together with the comments made by observers orally or in written form in English or in French according to the level of the learners. Suggestions as to appropriate alternatives and improvements should then be encouraged. Finally, the group should discuss whether it would be worth repeating the activity in similar or alternative form and, if so, which amendments are to be made.

MOTIVATING ASPECTS OF ROLE ACTIVITIES: SOME PREREQUISITES AND SUGGESTIONS

The selected roles and interactions must be perceived by learners to have relevance and point. Ideally, they should not be limited to, say, mundane transactions – which can become boring – and at least occasionally learners should be encouraged to engage in more imaginative situations, such as trying to persuade someone to buy or do something about which they have reservations. The programme of role activities should be varied to appeal to a range of interests within the group, both in the interactions selected and in the warm-up activities. In school, care should be taken to avoid an imbalance of adult contexts – especially if these do not include at least one role for a young person. Whatever the focus, learners should assume and maintain their assigned or chosen roles.

Ideally, the teacher should aim progressively to combine a variety of ready-made transactional roles with opportunities for the learners to tailor their own personalised roles in transactions constructed by themselves, with guidance and feedback from the teacher as required. Gradually, learners should be able to cope with increasing confidence with the 'unexpected', non-predicted and unscripted aspects of role interactions.

Each individual brings a unique learner's history to the group which will shape his or her interests, needs and preferences, and these should be drawn upon appropriately to construct, in collaboration with the teacher, partner, small groups and the whole group, various roles and interactions of personal significance to learners. In developing this, the teacher should continually make learners aware of the need to specify cultural language and non-language components of the interaction, its roles and context, and to see it whole with its performance in mind.

This raising-to-consciousness of the key features of appropriate role contexts should in turn encourage and enable learners to reflect on and evaluate in an informed manner their own performances in role. It is not possible to cover more than a representative selection of role contents in any course design, but such practice should give learners opportunities to develop not only their repertoire of 'scripts' but also their ability to 'cope' with other contexts. Learning to behave 'in role', as such, is as important as learning the selected roles.

It is important to maintain a lively pace, and the teacher's expectations of this should be made explicit. One way of evaluating progress in role activities is in terms of the relative time taken by learners to enact a role or roles. If an enactment is unduly laboured, it often denotes under-preparation in terms of the language and behaviours necessary and/or insufficient briefing as to the content and expectations. The effects can be very demoralising. Used judiciously, a large, clearly visible stop-clock, preferably with an alarm, can energise dramatically the pace of language learning in general and role activities in particular. Learners can enjoy working purposefully 'in role' against the clock – often to the delight of their colleagues!

A good balance of praise and critical feedback by the teacher and observers is essential. It is important to approve the good points and to suggest positive alternatives when drawing attention to points for improvement. It also helps greatly to model the suggested versions and to encourage learners to try them quickly in the course of the feedback – taking care not to be sidetracked into too much detail in any one aspect.

Learners must be able to depend on a well-managed classroom – where role activities are not seen as an invitation to misbehave. The aim should be *jeu de rôle* rather than *jeu drôle* – unless the latter is intended! This does not mean that role activities should not be enjoyable – but for most learners they will tend to be more so if the learning environment is secure and supportive and they do not feel 'at risk' of ridicule and censure. The teacher should be in clear but unobtrusive command, and the expectation that learners remain 'on task' should be explicit. Special encouragement should be given to shy or reluctant pupils – some find the idea of role activities daunting, and it often assists if the teacher partners such pupils initially to provide additional support. Conversely, the extrovert volunteer should not always be allowed to go first!

What of those not directly involved in the actual performance of role activities? The role of observer–evaluator is one which should be specified, encouraged and developed with learners from an early stage – with adequate time scheduled for them to contribute positively to the feedback, and to suggest and demonstrate appropriate alternatives. Where appropriate, and within the range of learners' abilities, opportunities should be given to learners to take the roles of presenter, narrator, debriefer.

Over-repetition of a particular interaction should be avoided as this can quickly degenerate into a perfunctory ritual in which learners progressively see little point. Such non-interactions can quickly begin to de-sensitise learners and cause them to lose interest in, and enthusiasm for, such activities, whereas even a slight variation requires them to adjust with understanding their behaviour to realise a new outcome. Building into role activities challenging shifts of emphasis to encourage learners to scan and actively choose language skills, communicative behaviours and strategies from their repertoire of 'scripts' is a key function of the teacher.

Great care should be taken to establish a credible psychological environment/context. If the interaction takes place *au marché*, it helps considerably to set up the classroom accordingly and to have on hand appropriate realia – *la balance, des légumes, des vêtements*, etc; if *à la gare* – *des billets, des plans, des affiches*, etc. Explain to learners – as far as possible in the foreign language – the layout of the context: where the actors will enter, where they will move to, how they will exit, the noises of the context, traffic, shoppers, commuters, etc. The London Borough of Havering has created a Europa Centre in the form of a simulated European village. All the facilities are stocked with authentic goods and effects and staffed by trained native speakers. Language learners can visit the village and interact with the inhabitants of the village as they shop, visit the cinema, go to the bank, return faulty goods previously purchased, order a meal, book a holiday, chat over a Perrier at the Europa café, etc., wholly in the target language. Learners find it easier to interact in role in a supportive simulated environment.

On a reduced scale, the modern communicative foreign language class-room might provide simulated micro-contexts of the target culture adapted in accordance with particular contextual, thematic or functional foci. French notices, French money, French newspapers all contribute to the 'reality' of a simulated environment within which it is easier for learners to perform 'in role'. Within this cultural island, learners should be encouraged to behave in the ways of the target culture – with French gestures, hesitation phenomena, etc. Learners should be discouraged from enacting roles sitting at desks or tables unless the role demands this. Normally they will be moving about, developing with the guidance of the teacher or perhaps the foreign language assistant, synchrony of gesture or mien with the spoken word, in question or exclamatory form, within appropriate interactions; in short, behaving in French rather than merely mouthing French words.

The teacher should regularly focus learners' attention on the *inter*action of role activities – the need for players to collaborate, to monitor, relate and adjust to the perceived intentions of their partners, to understand and sustain words, actions, moves and the essentially complementary reciprocal and interconnected nature of role interactions. This involves not just acting but reacting and interacting. This entails complex, engaging, involving, purpose-ful behaviour – which is why the focus cannot be just on remembering and saying aloud an allotted piece of verbal language. 'Only connect!' would be a suitable slogan for role activities in the foreign language classroom.

CONCLUSION

In a properly planned programme of role activities the learners should be helped to gain increasing understanding and mastery of the dynamic interplay of the contents, contexts, means and manners involved in language as communicative behaviour and, by stages, to play, take, negotiate roles – that is, to behave appropriately in the foreign language. Such a programme can be genuinely educative both for learners and teacher in extending their understanding of human communication and behaviour. Shakespeare observed that, 'All the world's a stage' and that each of us plays many parts. In an increasingly international context, purposeful role activities in the foreign language classroom can contribute powerfully to extending the learners' awareness of their world and of the many roles they may come to play.

REFERENCES

Athay, M. and Darley, J. (1981) 'Social roles as interaction competencies', in W. Ickes and E. Knowles *Personality roles and Social Behaviour*, New York: Springer-Verlag.

Barnes, D., Briton, J. and Rosen, H. (eds) (1969) *Language, the Learner and the School*, Harmondsworth: Penguin.

Gumperz, J. (1966) 'The ethnology of linguistic change', in V. Bright (ed.) *Sociolinguistics*, The Hague.

Joy, B.K. (1987) 'The Havering Europa Centre: a village with a difference', *Times Educational Supplement*, 13 November.

Littlewood, W. (1981) *Communicative Language Teaching: An Introduction*, Cambridge: Cambridge University Press.

Livingstone, C. (1983) *Role Play in Language Learning*, Harlow: Longman.

Loveday, L. (1982) *The Sociolinguistics of Learning and Using a Non-Native Language*, Oxford: Pergamon Press.

Milroy, E. (1982) *Role-Play: A Practical Guide*, Aberdeen: Aberdeen University Press.

Schank, R. and Abelson, R. (1977) *Scripts, Plans, Goals and Understanding*, Hillsdale, N.J.: Erlbaum.

Zurcher, L.A. (1983) *Social Rôles: Conformity, Conflict and Creativity*, Sage Publications.

Acknowledgements

Chapter 1 'The historical ball and chain', © William Rowlinson, reprinted from *Personally Speaking: Teaching Languages for Use* (1985) by William Rowlinson, reproduced by permission of Oxford University Press.

Chapter 4 'The communicative approach and authentic texts', by David Little, Seán Devitt and David Singleton, from *Learning Foreign Languages from Authentic Texts: Theory and Practice*, Chapter 2, reproduced by permission of Authentik Language Learning Resources Ltd.

Chapter 5 'De l'imparfait du subjonctif aux méthodes communicatives: où en est l'enseignement des langues vivantes?', by Francis Debyser, from *Le Français dans le monde*, 196 (1985), reproduced by permission of the Editor.

Chapter 6 'Communication: sense and nonsense', by Michael Grenfell, from *Language Learning Journal*, 3 (1991), reproduced by permission of the Association for Language Learning.

Chapter 7 'Mistakes are the mistake', by Keith Morrow, from *What Do You Mean – It's Wrong?* (1990), edited by Brian Page, reproduced by permission of the Centre for Information on Language Teaching and Research.

Chapter 9 'Autonomy in language learning: some theoretical and practical considerations', by David Little, from *Autonomy in Language Learning* (1990), edited by I. Gathercole, reproduced by permission of the Centre for Information on Language Teaching and Research.

Chapter 10 'Teaching materials and methods', by Barbara Lee, Senior Research Officer, National Foundation for Educational Research, Slough, UK, from her *Extending Opportunities: Modern Foreign Languages for Pupils with Special Educational Needs* (1991), reproduced by permission of the National Foundation for Educational Research.

Chapter 11 From *Teaching and Learning Language* (1982), Chapter 3, by E.W. Stevick, reproduced by permission of Cambridge University Press.

Chapter 13 'Teaching grammar in the target language', by Theodore B. Kalivoda from *Hispania* 73 (1) (1990), reproduced by permission of the author and the American Association of Teachers of Spanish and Portuguese.

Chapter 14 'Why do I have to get it right anyway?', by Brian Page, from *What Do You Mean – It's Wrong?* (1990), edited by Brian Page, reproduced by permission of the Centre for Information on Language Teaching and Research.

Chapter 15 'Raising reading attainment in modern languages', by Paul McGowan and Maggie Turner, from *Language Forum*, 1 (1 and 2) (1993), reproduced by permission of the Editor.

Chapter 17 From *Drama Techniques in Language Teaching* (1978), Introduction, by A. Maley and A. Duff, reproduced by permission of Cambridge University Press.

Chapter 18 'Approche communicative: un second souffle?' by Jean-Marc Caré, from *Le Français dans le monde* 226 (1989), reproduced by permission of the Editor.

Notes on sources

Chapter 1 William Rowlinson (1985) *Personally Speaking: Teaching Languages for Use*, 2, Oxford, Oxford University Press.

Chapter 2 Commissioned for this volume.

Chapter 3 Commissioned for this volume.

Chapter 4 David Little, Seán Devitt and David Singleton (1989) *Learning Foreign Languages From Authentic Texts: Theory and Practice*, Chapter 2, Dublin, Authentik.

Chapter 5 Francis Debyser (1985) 'De l'imparfait du subjonctif aux méthodes communicatives', *Le Français dans le monde*, No. 196 (October).

Chapter 6 Michael Grenfell (1991) 'Communication: sense and nonsense', *Language Learning Journal* No. 3 (March).

Chapter 7 Keith Morrow (1990) 'Mistakes are the mistake', in B. Page (ed.) *What Do You Mean – It's Wrong?*, London, CILT.

Chapter 8 Commissioned for this volume.

Chapter 9 David Little (1990) 'Autonomy in language learning: some theoretical and practical considerations', in I. Gathercole (ed.) *Autonomy in Language Learning*, London, CILT.

Chapter 10 Barbara Lee (1991) *Extending Opportunities: Modern Foreign Languages for Pupils with Special Educational Needs*, Chapter 4, London, NFER.

Chapter 11 Earl W. Stevick (1982) *Teaching and Learning Languages*, Chapter 3, Cambridge, Cambridge University Press.

Chapter 12 Commissioned for this volume.

Chapter 13 Theodore B. Kalivoda (1990) 'Teaching grammar in the target language', *Hispania* 73(1).

Chapter 14 Brian Page (ed.) (1990) *What Do You Mean – It's Wrong?*, Chapter 7, London, CILT.

Chapter 15 An adapted version of this chapter can be found in *Languages Forum* 1 (1), February 1993.

Chapter 16 Commissioned for this volume.

Chapter 17 Alan Maley and Alan Duff (1978) *Drama Techniques in Language Teaching*, Introduction, Cambridge, Cambridge University Press.

Chapter 18 Jean-Marc Caré (1989) 'Approche communicative: un second souffle?', *Le Français dans le monde*, No. 226.

Chapter 19 Commissioned for this volume.

Index